BIRDING

for

BEGINNERS

A Comprehensive Introduction to the Art of Birdwatching

SECOND EDITION

SHEILA BUFF

Photographs by Richard Day

FALCONGUIDES

GUILFORD, CONNECTICUT
HELENA, MONTANA
AN IMPRINT OF GLOBE PEQUOT PRESS

FALCON GUIDES®

Copyright © 1993, 2010 by Sheila Buff

Copyright © 2010 Richard Day/Daybreak Imagery for all images except page 116 of Laughing Gull © Robert McKemie/Daybreak Imagery; page 115 of Laughing Gull © Susan Day/Daybreak Imagery; page 13 © Susan Day/Daybreak Imagery.

FalconGuides is an imprint of Globe Pequot Press.

Falcon, FalconGuides, and Outfit Your Mind are registered trademarks of Morris Book Publishing, LLC.

Project editor: David Legere
Text design: Sheryl P. Kober
Layout: Joanna Beyer

Library of Congress Cataloging-in-Publication Data is available on file.

ISBN 978-1-59921-914-1

Printed in China

10 9 8 7 6 5 4 3 2 1

The author and Globe Pequot Press assume no liability for accidents happening to, or injuries sustained by, readers who engage in the activities described in this book.

CONTENTS

INTRODUCTION

This is a book for beginning birdwatchers, written by someone who considers herself no more than an intermediate birder. So much of what experienced birders take for granted is brand new to beginners, who find themselves bewildered by jargon, mystified by basic identification, and frustrated by their inability to find birds to watch. The goal of *Birding for Beginners* is to present, in a calm and reassuring manner, the sort of basic information that people just getting started in birdwatching need.

As so many birding books inexplicably do, this book has a bias toward the northeastern United States. More specifically, it is biased toward the Hudson Valley, where the author does most of her birdwatching. Although the examples tend to be based on the birds common there, the basic principles should be universally applicable. The great Louis Pasteur, originator of the modern scientific method, once said, "In the fields of observation, chance favors the prepared mind." If you understand the simple logic of bird families, habitats, and field observation, you will see more birds and identify them more readily.

The chapters of this book are arranged in a sequence appealing to the perspective of someone very new to birdwatching. Thus, the book begins not with identification techniques but rather with a chapter on simply finding birds to identify. From there it discusses that essential tool, the field guide. Basic information on bird identification through appearance, song, habitat, and behavior is found in chapters 3 through 6; the joys and pitfalls of listing are discussed in chapter 7. Chapter 8 is a long but important chapter on optics for birders. In chapter 9, the basics of an enjoyable day in the field are covered. The last chapter and the appendices detail how and where to learn more about birds. Birders tend to be systematic and logical, but there is no particular need to read this book in chapter order.

Beginners, especially those taking up the pursuit of birds as older adults, need to keep their perspective. What matters on a birding trip is not that you see a lot of different or unusual birds or that you see more of them than anyone else—what matters is that you have an enjoyable time appreciating the natural world. Improved identification skills and a longer life list will come naturally as you gain experience. In the meantime, do the best you can and have fun.

Of all the many satisfactions that birdwatching offers, perhaps the most profound is an intense appreciation of the vast, enormously complex web of nature. In recent years, birders have become deeply aware of how easily the fragile fabric of that web can be irreparably torn. The birds that were once so abundant in North America that passing flocks darkened the skies are today vanishing with distressing speed, victims of climate change and habitat destruction both here and in Central and South America. As the birds disappear, our natural heritage of beauty and life is also being destroyed forever. If we are to have birds to watch in the future, we must act now to preserve the planet we share with them.

1

FINDING AND
WATCHING BIRDS

The most important requirement for becoming a proficient birdwatcher is something you have already: enthusiasm for the natural world. All you need to do is take that enthusiasm, grab your binoculars, step outdoors, and start looking.

BIRDS ALL AROUND

As you get started in birdwatching, you may come to the startling realization that you have always been surrounded by birds and never really knew it. The simplest way to find birds to watch is to look in your own backyard. In a typical urban or suburban yard (or park or other open area), you will routinely see several obvious and easily identified common species, including House (English) Sparrows, Rock Doves (pigeons), starlings, robins, Blue Jays, and perhaps a few more.

If you put up a birdfeeder or a birdbath, you will attract more and different birds to observe. But doesn't that mean that the birds were there all along? Yes—you simply weren't looking for them. Now that you know they're there, practice your birding techniques on them.

One really satisfying aspect of birdwatching is that the more you watch, the more you see. The more often and more carefully you look at the familiar birds in your backyard, the

The American Robin, with its orange-red breast and erect posture, is one of the most familiar of birds, often seen on suburban lawns. It is so familiar, in fact, that it is frequently used as a reference bird—other birds are compared with it in terms of size or song. The typical robin stands about 10 inches tall.

better you will get to know them and how they behave. You may learn even to recognize individual birds among several of the same species. You will also start to see additional species because you have learned to differentiate among similar birds. For example, the small, brownish birds that you previously lumped together as just sparrows will resolve themselves into distinct species. And when a slightly different sparrow-like bird turns up, you will realize that it is a new bird for you, and you will be able to pin down its identity.

Most amazing of all, new birds will seem to occur more often because you have begun to look more carefully at all the birds you see.

The most common birds are also the most important to know really well because they are often the benchmarks for descriptions and comparisons. Birds are often described as being about the size of a sparrow, robin, crow, or other common bird, for example. The better you know the common birds, the better you will be able to identify related birds and the better you will understand the differences among birds. The same behavior patterns you see in backyard birds can be seen, with minor variations, in birds anywhere. After you learn to recognize aggressive behavior in a Tufted Titmouse at your feeder, for example, you will probably be able to recognize that behavior in other birds in different feeding situations.

HABITAT AND NICHE

Moving beyond your immediate neighborhood, where are the birds? Try looking in any open area with vegetation, especially one with water: fields, vacant lots, parks, wooded areas, streambeds, and fields near airports. Even if you live in an urban area, there's bound to be some open space around you. Central Park, in the heart of densely urban Manhattan, is an oasis for birds. More than 250 species have been sighted there, while more than 300 species have been seen at Jamaica Bay Wildlife Refuge, quite literally in the shadow of Kennedy International Airport. Today, due to recovery efforts over the past few decades, Peregrine Falcons feed on complacent pigeons and nest successfully on skyscrapers, bridge towers, power plant smokestacks, and similar artificial cliffs in many urban locations, including the Brooklyn Bridge.

Going a little farther afield, get to know the more obscure corners of your area. Abandoned railroad tracks, landfills and dumps, sewage treatment plants, and other attractive (to birds) sites are excellent places for spotting birds. Admittedly, breathing in the aroma of a sewage settling pond is not everyone's idea of a good time, but don't let peer pressure stop you. Look forward to the time when you can visit the Brownsville dump in the Rio Grande Valley to see Mexican Crows.

What are you really doing as you wander around town peering into drainage canals and gazing up into trees? You are looking for birds in a variety of ecological habitats and niches—and the more habitats and niches you explore, the more birds you will see.

The concepts of range, habitat, and niche are crucial to finding and understanding birds. Broadly speaking, the range is the geographic area in which a species is found. Some species are resident year-round in their range; migratory birds have winter and breeding ranges. Within the range, birds occupy habitats and ecological niches.

A bird's range often encompasses a variety of geographic features and plant communities. Within its range, a particular bird will usually be found only in its preferred habitat or a particular combination of terrain and vegetation. Some birds are commonly found in broadly defined habitats such as mixed deciduous woodlands; others are found only in very restricted habitats such as large stands of jack pines, 6–18 feet tall, in north-central Michigan (the rare Kirtland's Warbler).

Within a habitat, particular birds can reliably be found occupying particular niches. A bird's niche is the role it plays within the habitat: where and how it lives, nests, finds food, and does everything else. The classic example of how niches work is the bill length of various shorebirds. Sanderlings, which have short, slightly stubby bills, are found in the same habitat as Long-billed Curlews, which have long, slender bills some 9 inches long. These birds can share the same habitat because they occupy different niches within it: The sanderling feeds on tiny crustaceans it finds just below the surface of the sand right where the waves wash in and out; the Long-billed Curlew feeds on worms it pulls from deep burrows in mud flats.

From the preceding discussion, it is clear that different birds are found in different habitats and that the way to find birds to watch is to visit their habitats. The area where habitats come together—where woodland meets with open fields, for example—is called an "ecotone." Because ecotones contain mixed habitats, they also contain mixed bird life. Thus, ecotones tend to have more birds of more species than do individual habitats. Among birders, this is known as the "edge effect." One good way to see more birds is to seek out edges and mixed habitats.

WHERE TO GO

Fortunately for birdwatchers and other nature lovers, North America contains a wide variety of easily accessible habitats open to the public. The birds are found in the thousands of parks, wildlife refuges and reserves, wilderness areas, bird sanctuaries, and other natural spots at the national, state, provincial, and municipal levels. In addition, sanctuaries and refuges covering thousands of acres are owned and operated by nonprofit organizations such as the National Audubon Society and the Nature Conservancy.

A really good way to see birds in the company of more experienced birdwatchers is to join your local birding club. The friendly and enthusiastic members of the club will have regularly scheduled evening meetings devoted to slide shows, discussions, and the occasional guest speaker; they will also have regularly scheduled field trips to local sites. Bird clubs also often organize field trips to more distant places, arranging for carpools or buses and lodging.

If you are new to birding, you may not know if there is a club in your area, but there almost certainly is. A simple Web search will probably turn up at least one nearby group; you can also check the Web site of the American Birding Association or birdingguide.com. Simply asking around, noticing announcements of bird walks in the local paper, and calling your local county extension agent or fish and wildlife department will also work. Even if you can't find a club in your area, the staff members at local parks, refuges, preserves, and other open space sites often organize guided bird walks. This is a good, inexpensive way to learn more about birds and get connected with local nature lovers.

One of the very best ways to see a lot of different birds in a short time is to visit a birding hot spot during migration periods. Hot spots are places where birds congregate in large numbers and in great variety. An internationally famous hot spot is Cape May in New Jersey. During the spring and autumn migrations, many birds follow the Atlantic coast flyway. If they are headed south, they often land at Cape May at the tip of New Jersey to rest, feed, and await favorable weather before taking off to cross the open water of Delaware Bay. Conversely, if they are headed north, the birds land at Cape May after flying over Delaware Bay.

There are numerous other hot spots in North America, as well as thousands of other good places to bird. Books discussing—often in very specific detail—places to go and what you are likely to see are called "finding guides." On the local level, finding guides may cover only a county or even just a municipality. Guides detail good birding sites for virtually every state and province, while additional guides cover regions such as New England or the lower Colorado River valley. An excellent selection of finding guides is available through the American Birding Association (see Appendix B). Today many states with good birding, such as Texas, Arizona, Virginia, Alabama, and others, have organized birding trails that link preserves, refuges, and other sites. Even regions within states and individual

NATIONAL WILDLIFE REFUGES

The amazing National Wildlife Refuge (NWR) System began in 1903, when President Theodore Roosevelt designated Florida's Pelican Island as the first wildlife refuge. Today the system is managed by the U.S. Fish and Wildlife Service and has grown to more than 150 million acres, 550 national wildlife refuges and other units, plus 37 wetland management districts. Any NWR site is by definition a great place to find birds. To find sites near you, check www.fws.gov/refuges.

BIRDING BUSINESS

Birdwatching is big business. According to U.S. Fish and Wildlife Service surveys, in 2006 there were 48 million birders age sixteen or older in the United States—about 21 percent of the population. The surveys use a very conservative definition. To be counted as a birder, an individual must have either taken a trip 1 mile or more from home for the primary purpose of observing birds and/or have closely observed or tried to identify birds around the home. Leaving out backyard birders, more than 20 million birders travel to see birds every year. In 2006 trip-related and equipment-related expenditures by birders generated over $82 billion in total industry output, 671,000 jobs, and $11 billion in local, state, and federal tax revenue. Not surprisingly, many states with good birding opportunities have realized that visiting birders bring in substantial revenue and make special efforts to attract birders with birding trails, festivals, and other activities. Check with the tourism office for any state you're planning to visit—chances are that you'll find a lot of information aimed at birders and nature lovers, including free maps, brochures, and listings of events.

counties and municipalities have trails or guides listing good birding spots. Detailed information about trails and birding in the area can generally be found on tourism-oriented Web sites for the state or region; state fish and wildlife Web sites also have a lot of great information. The sites usually let you download or request brochures and maps. An up-to-date state trail list is found on the American Birding Association Web site.

When you arrive at a birding site—a wildlife refuge, for example—always stop first at the visitors' center, where you may pay an entrance fee or make a modest contribution, get a checklist and a map (usually free or at nominal cost), and chat with anyone who is there. Ask about what birds are being seen in various locations. If there is a sighting book, take a look at the entries from the past few days. Other birding visitors may have noted interesting birds and where they were seen. Finally, always use the restroom facilities—there probably won't be any in the field.

SPOTTING BIRDS

Beginners often don't see many birds even when they get to where the birds are. The birds are there—you just need some basic pointers and a lot of practice.

Start by simply trying to *see* birds—not necessarily to identify them. Go birdwatching when the birds are most likely to be active: the first few hours from dawn on or the last couple of hours before dusk. In woods, fields, and parks, on paths and along roadsides, walk slowly and quietly, holding your binoculars lightly with both hands. Avoid making sudden movements, pointing, and making loud noises. Keep alert for telltale motion in the vegetation. If you see some leaves rustle or catch the motion of a flitting bird out of the corner of your eye, stand still and look carefully at the suspect area. If you see the bird or see movement, keep your eyes fixed on the spot. Bring your binoculars up to your eyes with both hands and focus. If you can't see the bird but are sure you are focused on the right spot (more or less), scan back and forth around the area, starting at the top and working your way down. (Don't scan in circles—you'll make yourself dizzy.) The chances are good that the bird is still somewhere nearby. On the other hand, there's a reasonable chance that what you saw was simply the very common falling-leaf bird. In that case, it's time to move on, especially if you're not also hearing any bird sounds.

You will need to practice the technique of bringing your binocs up smoothly without taking your gaze off the bird. To avoid serious frustration, practice this assiduously at your backyard feeder or on the pigeons in a park until it becomes second nature.

If you think you are scaring the birds away, try disguising your presence by leaning against a tree trunk or squatting behind a bush. Don't give up too quickly—if you want to see the bird, you may have to wait several minutes or even longer. On the other hand, don't linger too long if you're pretty sure the bird has flown or if you start to feel your frustration level rising.

Listen for birdsongs and calls; also listen for rustling and scratching noises. Particularly in the spring, birds often perch on high points to proclaim their territories (a classic example is a meadowlark singing from a fencepost in a field). If you hear a bird, stand still and try to pinpoint the sound or at least its general direction. Scan the area with your binocs and try to spot the bird. If you hear a song, scan projecting branches, the tops of trees and bushes, fence posts, and overhead wires. If you hear calls or feeding noises (the sound of a towhee scratching up dead leaves on the forest floor, for example), scan lower down. Often a bird stops singing or calling when it sees people.

If this happens, stand still and wait. The bird will very likely resume singing in a few minutes. After you've spotted a singing bird, keep looking. Other birds—particularly a female of the same species—may be nearby.

Check around ponds, lakes, and wet, brushy areas such as streambeds—the trees and vegetation can abound in warblers in the spring, and birds such as Spotted Sandpipers and Louisiana Waterthrushes can often be found on the ground.

Look up. Scan the sky for hawks and other birds. Scan overhead wires, poles, and rooftops. It is astonishing how many people never notice anything that is above eye level unless it is specifically pointed out to them. (Black Vultures by the dozen can be seen perched broodingly on the roof of the huge vehicle assembly building at the Kennedy Space Center, yet busload after busload of tourists fails to notice them.) Try to follow the paths of flying birds and note where they alight. Often a flying bird moves only a short distance. It may flit from one branch to another or dart out to grab an insect and return to its original spot or one nearby. As you scan the sky or follow the movement of a flying bird, be aware of the sun's location. Don't look at the sun through your binoculars.

Always look carefully at *all* the birds in a group or flock of birds. A small flock of one warbler species may have a few other warblers or other birds mixed in; a group of what seem to be identical sandpipers may, in fact, contain several species.

In woodlands and fields, you can try another technique: Let the birds come to you. Dress warmly—you will be sitting still for a long time. Bring along something waterproof to sit on, something to drink, your binoculars, and your notebook. Find a likely spot—an open area at the base of a large tree, for example—and settle down to see what comes your way. After you have been sitting quietly for five or ten minutes, the birds will begin to go about their business while ignoring you. Within twenty minutes, you could easily find yourself looking a chickadee or a Yellow Warbler in the eye.

Shorebirds and waterfowl in wetlands and coastal regions are a little easier to spot because they are usually out in the open. The best way to see these birds is to visit a refuge area. Many of these sites have trails, roads, or boardwalks specifically designed to provide good viewing with a minimum of effort. Many sites have loop roads that let you drive conveniently from turnout to turnout. Your car is actually an excellent bird blind, making this the easiest sort of birding and ideal for people with mobility handicaps.

To see shorebirds when they are feeding and most active, try to time your visit to coincide with low tide, when mud flats and the beach are exposed. At high tide, the birds tend to huddle together and not do much of anything. To plan your trip efficiently, check with the site in advance for tide information or go to the tides and currents section of the National Oceanic and Atmospheric Administration (NOAA) Web site at tides andcurrents.noaa.gov/.

In addition to looking for birds swimming in the water or standing on the mud flats or shoreline, be sure to scan the tops of the vegetation for songbirds. Scan along the base of the phragmites for elusive birds such as rails. (Phragmites, or "phrags" for short, are the very tall, dense, reedy grass with a

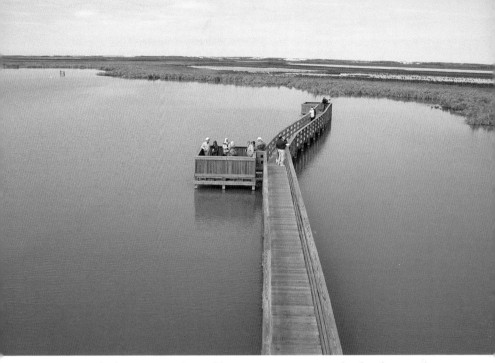

Here is birding at its simplest and least strenuous—viewing the abundant birdlife in a wetland from a convenient, sturdy boardwalk. This is a great way to avoid the newbie frustration of not being able to find birds to watch.
COURTESY OF SUSAN DAY/DAYBREAK IMAGERY

feathery top that makes up the dominant vegetation at many wetlands sites.)

If the site has an observation tower, climb it. This is a good way to grasp the lay of the land, watch birds in flight, see birds that are floating offshore, and appreciate the size of large flocks of birds.

Some sites have blinds (also called hides) set up at convenient observation points. The shelter of a blind is particularly welcome in windy and wet weather. Blinds are useful whenever concealment is needed for spotting shy birds, watching nest sites, and the like. When you are inside a blind, stay back a bit from the viewing window—the birds will see you if you put your face directly into the opening. If the blind is already occupied, politely ask if there's room for another person. If not, leave and come back later—your presence outside the blind will scare away the birds. Move and speak quietly. Be sure to close the window covers and door properly when you leave and obey any other injunctions that may be posted in the blind.

Pishing

All too often, the birds you want to see are lurking out of sight, hidden in foliage or undergrowth. You can often get the birds to appear, at least briefly, by making noises to attract them.

Pishing (or spishing) is the technique of attracting birds with a rhythmic hissing, "pishing," or "spishing" noise made by inhaling and exhaling loudly through closed teeth while simultaneously moving the lips. At its tamest, pishing sounds much like the hissing noise customarily used to call cats. Enthusiastic pishers manage to produce a loud, wheezy, sustained noise with lots of harmonic overtones in it. One word of advice: Don't talk about pishing into the bushes in polite (i.e., non-birding) company.

To pish effectively, position yourself inconspicuously near a likely spot—a brushy area near a stream, for example. Pish loudly and long, keeping the noise up for several minutes or until you run out of breath and get dizzy. Especially during migration periods, you are likely to attract birds of several species to the area around you. Some birds respond better than others to pishing. Chickadees, catbirds, kinglets, nuthatches, sparrows, thrushes, and warblers are particularly quick to respond, but other birds such as jays and woodpeckers may also appear. Pishing is an excellent way to get the warblers that are darting around in the woods and undergrowth to pop out where they can be seen. You will hear alarm chirps and rustlings and then start seeing the birds. Have your binoculars at the ready.

An alternative to pishing is to make squeaking or smacking sounds with your lips against the back of your hand or the tips of two fingers. Try to make the squeaks high pitched and alarmed sounding.

The terminally self-conscious can make squeaks and alarm calls using an ingenious little device called an Audubon Bird Call. Consisting of a pewter plug that rotates inside a small wooden tube, the caller produces a variety of squeaky noises. In practiced hands, surprisingly realistic imitations of birdsongs are possible. Audubon Bird Calls are very inexpensive; they are easily found in nature stores and mail-order catalogs.

Exactly why birds respond to pishing and squeaking is not fully understood. The most likely explanation is that the birds interpret the sounds as the distress call of a bird under attack from a predator and react accordingly. You will notice that the birds you attract by pishing often give their alarm calls in response. Pish judiciously to avoid stressing the birds. Stop pishing after the birds respond—this makes them think they have been successful in chasing off the predator.

Just as birds respond to pishing, they will respond to the sound of an owl's call by attempting to mob the predator. You can easily imitate the whinnying call of an Eastern Screech Owl, or you can play back a recording of the sound. As with pishing, use owl calls judiciously to avoid stressing the birds. Select a likely spot, play the recording for just a minute or so, and wait several minutes for the reaction. If you don't get a response, move on. If birds do come in, as with pishing, you must let the birds think they have chased the predator away. Move on to another spot a good distance away before you play the recording again. *Never* play an owl recording in the territory of an endangered species. In fact, never play an owl recording if you have the slightest doubt about whether it could be harmful to the birds you're trying to attract.

To attract a particular bird, you could imitate its song. Most people aren't very good at this, however, and prefer to play recordings instead. Male territorial birds will respond to imitations or recordings with alacrity because they think another bird has invaded their territory. Recordings in particular must be used with great caution. Simply by imitating a birdsong or playing a recording of it, you create unnatural stress for the bird because you cause it to respond to a nonexistent threat. The more you play the recording, the more stress you cause. Turn off the recording as soon as you get a glimpse of the bird and don't use it again in that bird's territory. Some refuges now ban the use of recordings entirely because overenthusiastic birders have caused nest failures and other problems by playing recordings to excess. Use recordings sparingly and ethically.

WEATHER AND SEASON

As a birder, you need to be very aware of the weather because is has a major impact on the birds you see. The five-second weather summary on the local radio station, or even the longer weather report on the local television station, is no longer sufficient. Go online to sites such the National Weather Service (nws.noaa.gov), Weatherbug (weather.weatherbug.com), or the Weather Channel (weather.com)—the detailed, accurate, and frequently updated reports for the area you are visiting will help you plan your trip and dress appropriately for the weather.

Moderately bad weather doesn't necessarily mean bad birding, at least from the birds' perspective. Severe weather, such as extreme cold or heat, heavy rain or snow, or heavy winds, will make the birds slow their activity and take shelter.

Bird migration is closely tied to weather fronts. In particular, wind can have a powerful effect. Migrants flying north over large bodies of water (the Gulf of Mexico, for example) sometimes encounter bad weather and adverse winds as they near the land. Because the exhausted birds can't fight their way inland against the wind, they come down onto the first land they see. In birder parlance, this is called a "fallout," and it is a bonanza. The birds are everywhere and are so tired they can hardly move. Fallouts occur with some regularity at predictable places such as Cape May in New Jersey, High Island near Galveston, Texas, Dauphin Island on the Alabama coast, or Point Pelee in Ontario on Lake Erie.

Conversely, migrating birds sometimes encounter unfavorable conditions and adverse winds as they prepare to cross a large body of water. Again, the birds back up, sometimes in spectacularly large numbers, while they wait for conditions to improve.

When bad weather clears up, migrating birds move again. The result can be a wave of birds passing through. One of the most delightful sights for a birder is a wave of colorful warblers in bright spring plumage. The numbers and variety that can be seen in a warbler wave will absolutely astonish you the first time you experience it.

In the autumn, the weather has a significant effect on bird movements. This effect can be seen most profoundly in the case of hawk migration. Because these soaring birds count on thermal currents of warm air, their migration tends to stall when the weather gets cold and rainy. After a few chilly, wet days, a clear, sunny day will bring the hawks down the migration route in large numbers. Cold fronts and low-pressure zones tend to push migrating birds ahead of them; sometimes the passage of large numbers of migrants presages the arrival of significantly colder and nastier weather.

Severe storms or hurricanes can blow birds far from their usual habitat. Offshore storms can drive pelagic (ocean-going) birds close to the shore, where they can be seen with spotting scopes. Shorebirds can be driven far inland. A bird found significantly off course in a place where it shouldn't be is called an "accidental" or a "vagrant."

In the spring, birds tend to sing less when the weather is cool and cloudy. Wet, windy weather tends to make birds clam up and disappear as they seek shelter. Sometimes the passing of a short rain squall can provide you with a birdwatching treat. The birds pop up singing all around you as the sun comes out again.

The easiest birdwatching for beginners probably happens in the spring, when the birds migrate north in large numbers starting as early as March. These birds are wearing their bright breeding plumage and singing loudly, making them easier to identify. In addition, most trees and other plants are just budding out and have not yet developed their full foliage, so the birds are easier to spot.

Birds tend to be much quieter and harder to spot in the summer, but some shorebirds complete their breeding and begin to migrate to their winter territories as early as mid-July. By the end of August, other birds are definitely on the move. Autumn migration tends to be more diffuse—there are no warbler waves, for example—but also more numerous because the young birds born that year swell the numbers heading south. Birds in autumn are more difficult to identify because, by this time, their breeding plumage has faded. In the winter, there are fewer bird species to see, but they are easier to spot because there is little foliage to get in the way. Put up a birdfeeder in the winter and get to know your backyard birds better. Winter also brings the occasional irruption, or large movement of birds into areas beyond their normal range. Irruptions generally occur when a species can no longer find food in its usual range. Irruptive species tend to be birds that depend on food sources that are subject to sudden crashes. When the population of voles and lemmings in the subarctic regions of Canada goes through one of its periodic crashes, for example, raptors such as Snowy Owls head south in search of food. Similarly, winter irruptions of Red and White-winged Crossbills are fairly common, probably due to a shortage of the coniferous seeds these birds eat. Irruptions are unpredictable and irregular; when one happens, word spreads quickly among the birding community.

BIRDING ETHICS

You are, of course, an ethical person in your daily life. You also, of course, wish to be an ethical birder. If you apply your usual high ethical standards to your birding, you can't go wrong. If you understand a few specific points, you will never be in doubt about acceptable birding behavior.

All native wild birds, with the exception of Rock Doves (pigeons), starlings, and House Sparrows, are protected by federal, state, and provincial laws. In essence, these laws forbid individuals from harming, killing, capturing, possessing, or otherwise hurting protected birds. The law extends to any parts of birds (feathers), bird nests, and eggs.

The preceding taboos were first set out on the federal level in the United States and Canada by the Migratory Bird Treaty Act of 1916; they have since been expanded and amended, most notably in the United States by the Endangered Species Preservation Act of 1966 and by the more comprehensive Endangered Species Act of 1973.

Theoretically, anyone found in possession of any wild bird or part thereof for any reason is breaking federal law (and probably state or provincial law as well) and can be imprisoned and fined. Aside from licensed hunting, there are some exceptions to the law. Permits are granted for scientific research, banding operations, and other legitimate pursuits. You are permitted to possess a wild bird in an emergency—bringing an injured hawk to a rehabilitation center, for example. It is unlikely, though theoretically possible, that you will be prosecuted for picking up a feather in the woods or bringing home an old nest, but think carefully before you do. Remember that in 1983 Dave Winfield, then an outfielder with the New York Yankees, was arrested after he accidentally killed a gull with a warm-up throw during a game in Toronto.

The Endangered Species Act and its amendments specifically prohibit you not only from possessing a bird but also from harassing it in any way, whether deliberately or unintentionally. This means that you are forbidden from doing anything that could cause the bird to change its normal behavior and thus endanger its welfare. You might naively think that no birder would ever harass a bird, particularly an unusual or endangered one, but this sort of behavior occurs among birders with depressing regularity. Rare birds, especially those found outside their usual range, can attract so many enthusiastic birders that the area becomes literally overrun, resulting in crowded trails, trampled vegetation, and serious disturbance to all the birds and wildlife. During the breeding season, the birds may be so disturbed that they abandon their efforts or delay them to the point where the chicks are born too late in the year to survive. The desire to add a rare bird to your life list can be very strong, but it is no excuse for unacceptable birding behavior.

Using a recording to attract birds can be a very effective but also a very controversial technique. Recordings must always be used in an ethical manner that avoids unnecessary stress on the bird. It is obviously unethical to use any recordings at all in the territory of endangered species. It is also obviously unethical to use recordings to excess. Less obviously unethical is causing the cumulative stress that can occur when different birders play recordings to the same birds. You may not feel that you are causing a bird much stress if you briefly play an owl recording to attract it. But what happens when fifteen minutes after you leave, another birder comes along and does the same thing, and another birder after that?

On the other hand, which is preferable: a group of five birders crashing through the undergrowth in pursuit of a bird or five birders waiting quietly on a trail and calling the bird to them briefly with a recording? Judicious use of a recording here is appropriate. Weigh the pros and cons carefully before playing a recording. If you have the slightest doubt, don't play it.

Trespassing is an act where situational ethics tend to apply. Birders should avoid trespassing on private property and posted lands. This rule can be flexible, however. Obviously, you should ask permission before entering someone's backyard, farmland, or posted land. On the other hand, say that an interesting bird presents itself while you are driving along a deserted road bordered by posted woods. Is it ethical to enter the woods to see the bird? You decide.

If you are birding by permission on private property, be courteous. In particular, stay on the paths and don't trample any vegetation or disturb any animals. Stay out of any fields with crops, including hay, and don't disturb any livestock. Don't enter fields with locked gates; leave other gates as you find them. Don't leave any trash behind. In residential areas, don't turn up at the crack of dawn or go prowling around in the evening. At best you will be considered a weirdo and a nuisance; at worst you could be mistaken for an intruder. Sometimes a rare bird will take up residence in the yard of a homeowner. When word gets out, birders descend on the area. Most homeowners in this situation are willing to accommodate birders, but again, be courteous and considerate. Ask permission, don't show up at odd hours, and don't hang around for hours. Park carefully and be sure to thank the homeowner on your way out.

It is your obligation as a birder to behave in an ethical manner and to make sure that others behave properly as well. Read carefully the American Birding Association's code of birding ethics in Appendix A and take it to heart.

2

GETTING AROUND YOUR FIELD GUIDE

The presence of a field guide is so well established today among birdwatchers that it is hard to imagine a time when these useful, compact volumes didn't exist. In fact, the birth of the modern field guide can be dated precisely to 1933, the year Roger Tory Peterson published his revolutionary book, *A Field Guide to the Birds,* illustrated with his own paintings.

THE FIELD MARK SYSTEM

Prior to Peterson, ornithologists generally described a bird by listing its characteristics literally from head to toe, giving equal weight to every aspect of the bird's outer physical appearance and usually including a detailed discussion of its internal structure as well. The exhaustive information was of very little help to anyone trying to identify a bird seen fleetingly in the field. And although the detailed and very accurate paintings of John James Audubon were available in cheap, poorly reproduced editions from about 1870 onward, these, too, were not particularly helpful for field identification.

The genius of Peterson was his brilliant system of identifying the birds by their field marks. Each description and painting points out the few significantly characteristic features of a bird that identify it as that species and no other. The Peterson field mark system was a radical change from those of all other field guides up to that time. Today the Peterson system is used by virtually all field guides to the birds and in most guides to other aspects of natural history.

Choosing a Field Guide

The latest iteration of *A Field Guide to the Birds,* or simply Peterson, came out in 2008. Instead of the previous eastern and western editions, the new edition covers all of North America in one volume. The new edition contains forty additional paintings by Michael O'Brien; Peterson's original paintings have been digitally enhanced. Peterson remains the standard by which all the numerous other field guides now available are judged. It is perhaps the best choice for a beginner simply because it is so readily available, so easy to use, and so familiar to the other birders you will encounter. Other field guides have their advantages, however, and most birders eventually end up owning at least two different volumes.

Several other excellent field guides are widely used. The classic *A Guide to Field Identification: Birds of North America* by Chandler S. Robbins, Bertel Bruun, and Herbert S. Zim, originally published by Golden Press, became *Birds: A Golden Guide* in 2001. Often called just the "Golden guide," this is still an excellent guide for beginning birders. So is the *National Geographic Field Guide to the Birds of North America.* An outstanding guide with excellent illustrations and text, along with lots of white space on the pages for making notes, this is the author's personal choice for new birders. The *National Wildlife Federation Field Guide to Birds of North*

America, illustrated with more than two thousand color photos and featuring a waterproof cover, is another good option. *The National Audubon Society Field Guide to North American Birds,* in eastern and western editions, is popular. Beginners may prefer a guide that covers only their region because it makes identification easier by listing only those birds found there. (Eastern and western North America is divided, somewhat arbitrarily, at the 100th meridian. A better way to think of the division is east and west of the Rockies.)

Another good choice for new birders is the *Smithsonian Field Guide to the Birds of North America,* illustrated with about two thousand color photos. The *Kaufman Field Guide to Birds of North America,* by renowned birder Kenn Kaufman, takes an interesting approach to the age-old debate about photos versus paintings in field guides by using digitally enhanced color photos to bring out the field marks for each bird.

In 2000 the birding world was rocked by the appearance of the magisterial *The Sibley Guide to Birds* by artist/author David Sibley. This volume is called a "field guide," but it is considerably too large and heavy for use in the field. For home use and study, *Sibley,* as it very quickly came to be called, is definitive, informative, and illustrated with exceptionally detailed and accurate paintings. No matter which field guide a beginning birder chooses, *Sibley* should be the backup. In 2003 compact editions of *Sibley,* for eastern and western America, were published. Using the same illustrations but with text and range maps more suited for field use, these smaller volumes are excellent choices for birders at all levels.

All of the preceding guides, with the exception of the Audubon Society and Kaufman volumes, are organized more or less taxonomically with an illustration near a written description of each bird. (See following for an explanation of taxonomy.) All include current range maps. Most have thumb tabs for quick reference. With the exception of the big Sibley volume, all are fairly compact and will fit easily into a large jacket or pack pocket. A serious drawback to the Audubon Society guide is that it is organized in a very peculiar manner. The front part of the book contains full-color photos of the birds cross-referenced to descriptions found separately in the back part of the book. To confuse matters further, the photographs are organized not by taxonomy but by broad categories such as gull-like birds. Within the categories, the photos are organized by the color of the bird. Within the written descriptions, the birds are again organized not by taxonomy but by habitat. This sort of arrangement may seem helpful at first because beginners often note only the most visible colors and have trouble deciding what family a bird belongs to, but it is fundamentally unsound and very unwieldy for field use.

Similarly, the Kaufman guide is organized by sixteen bird family groupings rather than by taxonomic order. It may be a bit easier for a new birder to identify a mystery bird by looking within the category "medium-sized land birds" or "chicken-like birds," but this approach will quickly become unsatisfactory after you have a better grasp of bird families.

Online field guides of various sorts are now common. An excellent multimedia online guide called "All About Birds," produced by the Cornell Laboratory of Ornithology, is found at allaboutbirds.org. There are many others—search to find sites you like.

USING YOUR FIELD GUIDE

The first step in using your field guide is buying it. Because you will be carrying the book around with you in the field, and because personal preferences regarding design and illustrations play a role in your choice, try to purchase your field guide from a brick-and-mortar bookstore. Seeing and holding the various guides will give you a sense of which will work best for you.

Buy only the most recent edition of a field guide. Do not use any musty old field guides you may find tucked away on a shelf of the summer cottage or in a box up in the attic. Ornithology is an ongoing science, and those guides will be out of date. The range maps in particular will almost certainly no longer be accurate.

Next, *read* the guide. This does not mean memorize all the descriptions. Rather, read the introduction and instructions on how to use the book. Get a feel for the book's organization and the way the information is presented. Learn how the range maps are set up and what any symbols mean. Browse through the pages and get to know the members of various bird families. Don't spend long periods reading one species description after another—you'll never remember the birds. Instead, spend fifteen minutes or so at a time studying a particular group of birds or working out which birds you are likely to see in a particular habitat.

Every field guide has a section, usually near the start, that describes the various parts of a bird, also known as "bird topography." This section generally uses a typical songbird, often along with a typical duck, to illustrate the various feather types and body features. Study this section to get an understanding of the terminology used for describing a bird's appearance. Terms such as "supercilium stripes," "malar patches," "lores," "median coverts," and so on all make sense after you're familiar with the topography section.

At first, finding a bird in your field guide will be a tedious exercise in page-flipping. As you become more familiar with the different bird families, you will be able to narrow the range of possibilities and turn to the most likely section(s) of the field guide quickly. After you can put a bird into its proper family (more or less), you will probably then be able to identify it specifically.

First, try to match the physical appearance of the bird to the illustration. Look for the field marks indicated in the illustration and described in the text. Compare your bird's actions with any behavior and habitat notes mentioned in the guide. Check the range map. If the bird had to be wildly off course to have ended up in your backyard, it's probably not the bird you think it is. Birds do sometimes end up doing uncharacteristic things in the wrong place, but, on the whole, they are surprisingly predictable.

After a while, your field guide will fall open at the right pages by itself—one sign that you have passed beyond the beginner phase. Until then, try putting paper clips on the pages you will refer to most on a birding trip. If you're visiting a coastal sanctuary, for example, put clips on the pages covering sandpipers and gulls.

Your field guide will be your constant companion both in the field and at home. It will gradually become scribbled in, bent, stained, and torn. You will develop an unreasonable sentimental attachment to it and secretly resent the appearance of a new edition. Worst of all, you will mourn if it is lost. Always write your name, address, and phone number in the front of your field guide. Birders understand how you feel and will make an effort to return a lost guide if they find one.

THE ART OF OBSERVATION

You love your field guide, and you depend on it. Is this a good thing? Maybe not—a field guide can be a crutch that substitutes for close observation. If you go into the field with your guide, you may develop a tendency to stop watching the bird too quickly while you look it up. You may have the satisfaction of identifying the bird, but, in the meantime, you may have missed some interesting behavior or some other birds. It's also quite possible that by simply observing the bird further—getting a better look at its appearance and behavior—you could arrive at an identification without relying on the field guide.

Try leaving your field guide behind or, if this makes you feel too insecure, bring it along and leave it in your pocket. Bring along a small, inexpensive, spiral-bound notebook and a strong rubber band to hold the page down. (Eventually, someone will give you a beautiful nature notebook made with exquisite paper and a sewn, hardcover binding. Thank the giver politely and put the notebook to some other use.) Also bring along two inexpensive, retractable ballpoint pens with clips (marker pens run on wet paper, pencil points break, and all pens get lost). When you spot an unknown bird, simply watch it carefully. In the case of small, fast-moving birds such as warblers or sparrows, make mental notes of the birds' appearance (this is one of many reasons birders talk to themselves); for larger birds such as ducks or herons, you can often scribble your notes as you watch. Make a sketch, no matter how rough or inept, of any interesting identification features, such as a crest on the head or the shape of the tail. Jot down anything else that might be useful for identifying the bird: an estimate of its size, habitat, and behavior. Make notes about any vocalizations you hear.

Upon returning home, study your notes and try to place the unidentified birds into the proper families. Next, make your best guess as to what species they are. Only then should you turn to your field guide to verify your identification.

Keeping field notes may be frustrating at first, particularly when you yearn for a life list in three figures. Stick with it. There's no better way to learn the art of observation than by doing it.

Your stained and tattered field notebooks will gradually fill up with observations, directions, phone numbers, restaurant recommendations, and cryptic notes that mean nothing to you three days later. Your notebooks contain your birding life—treasure them.

Bird Families and Bird Names

The basic concepts of taxonomy—the hierarchical classification of living things by their degree of common characteristics and evolutionary closeness—are crucial to birdwatching. By understanding taxonomy, you understand how the different bird species are related; after you understand the characteristics of a particular bird family, identifying individual species within the family becomes much easier.

The traditional first question in the game Twenty Questions asks "animal, vegetable, or mineral?" In the broadest taxonomic classification, birds belong to the animal kingdom. Moving down the hierarchy, birds belong to the phylum Chordata, or animals with a hollow dorsal nerve cord. Birds quite literally get into a class of their own—Aves—at the next level down. Here we have the taxonomic definition of a bird: a warm-blooded animal with feathers and wings that lays large, yolky eggs with chalky shells.

The class Aves is divided into about thirty orders, or groups of families. In scientific Latin, orders are indicated by the suffix "-iformes," which means "shape." Thus, the various vultures, hawks, and falcons are all members of the order Falconiformes (always capitalized, never italicized). The order Passeriformes is the largest order; it includes most of the birds more loosely referred to as "perching birds" or "songbirds." Orders are fundamental to bird identification—get to know them. Most field guides are organized by order, starting with the most primitive birds (loons) and ending with the most developed (sparrows). In taxonomic terms, "primitive" means simply oldest in the evolutionary sense.

Each order is divided into several families, indicated by the suffix "-idae." There are about 160 families altogether. Among the Falconiformes families are the Cathartidae (vultures), the Accipitridae (kites, hawks, eagles, and ospreys), and the Falconidae (caracaras and falcons). If you can classify a bird into its correct family, you have gone a long way toward identifying it. When discussing families within orders, field guides often make some changes in strict taxonomic sequence for the sake of clarity. Again, get to know the various families. You will often hear birders taking about larids, for example. If you have studied your field guide diligently, you will know they are referring to gulls.

Families are subdivided into subfamilies, indicated by the suffix "-inae." Among the family Accipitridae, for instance, are the subfamilies that include kites, accipiters, harriers, buteos, eagles, and ospreys. In some cases, subfamilies are further divided into tribes, indicated by the suffix "-ini." For example, there are four different tribes for North American ducks.

Next in the sequence comes the genus, or group of similar species. The genus (plural "genera") really helps you make sense of the larger families such as warblers because it combines them into manageable groups of birds that are related in appearance and behavior. A classic example of a genus with closely related birds is *Empidonax,* which contains a number of flycatchers that are almost identical in appearance and present a serious identification challenge. Birds belonging to the same genus are called "congeneric."

Finally, the field narrows to the fundamental unit of taxonomy: the species. A bird species is one that is closely related to other members of its genus but cannot interbreed with them. Every species is assigned a unique binomial (two-part name) in scientific Latin. These names stay constant even when a bird is known by two or more common names. For example, the American Woodcock is also sometimes called a "timber-doodle" or "bogsucker," but scientifically speaking it is always called "*Scolopax minor*." The first part of the binomial indicates the genus, always capitalized; the second part indicates the species, always lowercased. Species names are always italicized. After the genus has been given in full for the first time, it is often abbreviated to just its first letter (e.g., *S. minor*).

Some species have subspecies. A subspecies is a population of a species that shows some variation, often because of geographic separation, but has not evolved differences sufficient to prevent interbreeding. Subspecies are sometimes called "races." The Dark-eyed Junco (*Junco hyemais*) has at least six subspecies. The most easily observed are the Slate-colored race, common throughout Canada and the United States, and the Oregon race, common west of the Rockies. Slate-colored Juncos are a uniform gray color on the head, back, and breast; Oregon Juncos have a black breast and head and a rusty back.

Lumping and splitting

The basic hierarchical principles of modern taxonomy were laid down by the great Carl Linnaeus in 1735. Since then, advancing scientific knowledge has meant that bird classifications are sometimes revised—and then revised again—to reflect more accurately the relationships among species—a good reason to use an up-to-date field guide. A classic example was the decision in 1983 by the American Ornithologists' Union (AOU), the decisive authority for North and Central American bird

In 1983 the Baltimore Oriole and the Bullock's Oriole were lumped together as one species designated the "Northern Oriole." In 1995 the birds were split back into their original species. Splits and lumps in bird taxonomy happen fairly often—which is why you need to use an up-to-date field guide.

taxonomy, that the Baltimore Oriole of the east and the Bullock's Oriole of the west were really the same bird, to be called "Northern Oriole" (*Icterus galbula*), with Baltimore and Bullock's as subspecies. Further research showed that, in fact, these two birds are not even really that closely related, and they were restored as separate species in 1995. The Rufous-sided Towhee was split uncontroversially into the Spotted Towhee and the Eastern Towhee in 1995. In 1997 the Plain Titmouse was split into the Oak Titmouse and Juniper Titmouse. (Some birders proposed that better common names for these new species would be "Plain" and "Plainer Titmouse," but the ornithologists on the AOU nomenclature committee are very serious minded, and the suggestion was rejected. Look these birds up in your field guide to see why this is what passes for birding humor.)

When species are combined, they are said to be "lumped"; when species are divided, they are said to be "split." Needless to say, birders hate it when species are lumped because it deprives them of a bird on their life list. On the other hand, splits can add to your life list. Fierce controversy can surround taxonomic questions, and recent advances in DNA analysis are sure to add considerable fuel to the flames. For example, recent

WHO DECIDES?

The authoritative body for deciding bird taxonomy in North and Central America is the American Ornithologists' Union (AOU), which periodically updates its Checklist of North American Birds. Distinguished ornithologists on the AOU Checklist Committee review all the evidence for taxonomic and name changes and make their decision, which is then adopted worldwide. The changes are published every July as a supplement to The Auk, the official AOU journal. You can get the latest checklist of all 2,046 (and counting) North and Central American species online from the AOU at aou.org.

For birds worldwide, you have your choice of two standard lists. The first is Birds of the World: A Checklist by James F. Clements. Known simply as Clements, this is the official checklist of the American Birding Association. The other standard list is A World Checklist of Birds by Burt L. Monroe and Charles G. Sibley, known just as Sibley-Monroe.

DNA work suggests that New World vultures are more closely related to storks than to eagles and hawks. Even so, field guides continue to leave the vulture descriptions in their traditional place among the raptors, mostly because vultures look a lot more like raptors than like storks.

Every bird has a binomial scientific name, as explained earlier. Every bird also has an official common or vernacular name that is much easier to remember and pronounce. For example, *Dendroica petechia* is better known by the common name "Yellow Warbler." The common names are assigned by the American Ornithologists' Union and should always be capitalized in writing. Colloquial names are nonstandard names applied to a family, genus, or species. Colloquial names tend to be colorful but inexact. For example, "goonybird" is a colloquial name applied indiscriminately to albatrosses, and "whiskey Jack" is another name for the Gray Jay.

How do birds get their names? The scientific name is often descriptive of some aspect of the bird's appearance or behavior. Sometimes it commemorates an individual related to the bird in some way, and sometimes it doesn't seem to bear much relationship to anything. In Linnaeus's time, every educated person knew Latin and Greek and could understand what the scientific name meant, regardless of his or her native language. In our own very different time, few people study Latin and Greek, and the meaning of the scientific name is frequently incomprehensible. For translations, you can do your own detective work with an unabridged

dictionary or look the name up in one of the several diction-
aries of bird names.

Even if you can remember the scientific name, you may be
hesitant about pronouncing it. A good rule of thumb is just to
pronounce everything, including every vowel and letters at the
end of the name. The accent almost always falls on the next-to-
last syllable.

Common names, like scientific names, often describe
some obvious characteristic of the bird. This practice is helpful
both for remembering the name and for identifying the bird
because the name often points you toward a critical field mark.
Common names can sometimes be misleading, however. For
example, the Red-bellied Woodpecker does have a very faintly
pink abdomen, but the chief field marks for this bird are its
red cap and ladder back. Likewise, the Connecticut Warbler
is rarely found in that state. Sometimes the common name
commemorates an individual. The English naturalist William
Swainson (1789–1855) has three birds named in his honor:
Swainson's Hawk, Swainson's Thrush, and Swainson's Warbler. The lovely Anna's Hummingbird was named in honor
of Anna, wife of the Duc de Rivoli, a celebrated beauty in her
time (she died at the age of ninety in 1896). All told, seventy-
seven North American birds are named for people. John James
Audubon now has just one bird named in his honor: Audubon's Shearwater.

3

IDENTIFYING BIRDS

The core principle of birdwatching is identifying what you see, but bird identification is probably the most difficult and frustrating aspect of birding for beginners. How can you possibly be expected to know which sparrow you have just seen when, according to the field guide, it could be one of about twenty species?

OBSERVE AND IDENTIFY

The art and science of bird identification consist of observing as many features of the bird's appearance and behavior as possible, combining that information with observations of the season, habitat, and niche in which the bird is seen, and narrowing the range of possibilities down to a single species.

The basic skills of bird identification are not a mystery—they are easily learned by anyone. In fact, you can already identify several birds, and you already possess a good understanding of how to go about identifying birds you don't know. Think about the birds you already can identify. You know some by name: robin, Blue Jay, Mourning Dove, crow, mockingbird, and easily twenty or more additional species. You may not know some other birds by species, but you can accurately place them into their family: for example, sparrows, hawks, and gulls.

How do you know all this? Without digressing into a monograph on cognitive psychology, you can recognize some birds because they match the clear mental image you have developed over years of experience—you have been aware of the most familiar birds since childhood. Based on your fundamental knowledge of a few basic birds, you are able to categorize other birds into the appropriate family because you recognize the individual features that are characteristic of the family.

Just as you can recognize a good friend by seeing him or her from behind in a crowd of people, or by catching a glimpse of a characteristic gesture, or even by hearing a snatch of his or her laughter, so, too, can you learn to recognize birds at a glance.

Basic Identification Steps

Identifying a bird is basically a matter of systematic observation logically applied. Before you can do this, however, you need to be familiar with the concept of bird families and with the terminology that defines the various parts of a bird (see chapter 2).

The first step toward identification is to note the physical appearance of the bird. Next, whenever possible, watch it long enough to note aspects of its behavior. The section that follows concentrates on physical appearance; an extensive discussion of behavior watching is in chapter 5.

After you are focused in on a bird, run through a mental checklist of identifying features. The goal is to note the most obvious field marks and to arrive at a strong overall impression of the bird.

Color

The beautiful, vivid colors of some birds are often what attracts people to birding. Birds that are all or mostly one bright color are easy to identify. Their names are easy to remember because they usually incorporate a reference to the color. Examples include red birds such as cardinals and Scarlet Tanagers, blue birds such as Indigo Buntings and Eastern Bluebirds, and yellow birds such as American Goldfinches. For every bird that is easily identified by its highly visible color, however, many more are basically drab, with only touches of brighter color. In addition, the color of a bird can change with the season. American Goldfinches, for instance, are a bright yellow with glossy black wings in summer but drab khaki with dull black wings in winter.

The common name of the Gray Catbird gives two important clues to its identification: its overall gray color and its catlike mewing call. The black cap is another distinctive field mark.

Size

You already have a fairly good mental yardstick for noting the size of a bird. Simply compare it with a bird you know well. Is your mystery bird bigger than a generic sparrow but smaller than an American Robin? Is it about the size of a chickadee or a Rock Dove (pigeon)? Or is it really big, the size of a chicken or larger? It's much easier to use a comparison than it is to try to assign an actual numerical measurement. Size can sometimes be deceptive. A bird with fluffed-up feathers in cold weather looks larger than the same bird with sleeked-down feathers in warm weather. Poor lighting conditions also make it difficult

In the breeding season, the male American Goldfinch is bright yellow with black wings and a black forehead. The vivid yellow color and contrasting wings make this small, handsome bird unmistakable.

to estimate size. Size is also sometimes difficult to estimate through binoculars and spotting scopes. The compression caused by long optics can make a sparrow in the foreground look about the same size as a robin in the background. When estimating size, try to look at the bird both with the naked eye and with optics.

Shape

The overall shape of a bird is a very important clue. Birders use a variety of words to describe shape: "chunky," "trim,"

In nonbreeding (winter) plumage, the male American Goldfinch loses its distinctive markings. The body is an overall drab gray, the black cap is gone, and the black wings are brownish with tan wing bars.

"slender," "stocky," "plump," and "sleek." These terms are somewhat subjective because shape can't be defined exactly—it's more of an impression, and it can be affected by the bird's posture and activity. To get an idea of body shapes, compare the stocky shape of a Rock Dove with the slimmer body of a Mourning Dove.

The bill

If you can look at only one part of a bird, look at the head. Note particularly the shape and size of the bill and try to determine

The long, knifelike bill of the Green Heron is typical of the heron family. Herons are strictly carnivorous; their long bills are adapted to spearing and grasping fish, frogs, and other prey. Herons have S-shaped necks that let them dart their bills forward and strike with lightning swiftness.

its color (this is harder than it sounds). The bill is an excellent identification clue. Many birds or bird families take their name from the shape or color of the bill: tubenoses, shovelers, cross-bills, grosbeaks, Yellow-billed Cuckoos, Spoon-billed Ibis, and Ringed-bill Gulls. Bill shapes tend to be very similar within a bird family. Thus, all geese have broad, round-tipped bills; all warblers have thin, straight, pointed bills; all hummingbirds have long, slender bills; all herons have long, wicked-looking bills. A good look at the shape of the bill can do a lot to point you toward the right family.

The relative length of the bill is important when identifying birds such as sandpipers. For example, the Greater and Lesser Yellowlegs look much alike, but the bill of the Lesser Yellowlegs is slimmer and much shorter.

Bill color and markings are often hard to see. They're rarely an important field mark when identifying passerines, but they can be significant for other birds such as gulls and terns.

Generally, easily understood adjectives are used to describe bills. You do need to know the meaning of a few specialized bill terms:

- Beveled: the bill has a chisel-like tip (as in woodpeckers);

- Ceres: a leathery "saddle" at the base of the upper mandible (as in many raptors);

- Decurved: the bill curves downward (as in curlews);

- Frontal shield: a flat extension of the bill upward onto the forehead (as in coots and gallinules);

The strongly hooked bill of the Bald Eagle is typical of all acciptrids (hawks, eagles, and other members of the Accipitridae family). The bill is used to tear prey apart, not to catch it—acciptrids rely on their strong feet and very sharp talons to catch, kill, and carry prey.

Like all warblers, the Yellow Warbler has a slender, pointed bill ideal for finding and catching insects. A few warblers, such as the American Redstart, catch insects on the fly, but most glean insects, larvae, and eggs by foraging among twigs, leaves, bark, and buds.

- Recurved: the bill curves upward (as in avocets and some stilts);

- Serrate: the bill has "teeth" along the edges (as in mergansers); and

- Tubenose: external, tubular nostrils on top of the bill (as in albatrosses and shearwaters).

What's the difference between a bill and a beak? There really isn't any, but, for some reason, birders usually say "bill." Inexplicably, "beak" is generally reserved for raptors (birds of prey). The word "neb," meaning "bill," is reserved for crossword puzzles.

THE HEAD

Important field marks are found on the head, as the names of many birds suggest—Red-headed Woodpecker, for instance. Look particularly for solid colors, eye rings, eye stripes, crests, and head markings such as stripes, hoods, and masks.

The heads of some birds are a solid color that contrasts to the body color: Brown-headed Cowbird and Yellow-headed Blackbird are two self-evident examples.

An eye ring is an area of a contrasting color encircling the eye. Eye rings are sometimes partial or broken, and they are not always easy to see. Sometimes the eye ring can give the bird a big-eyed look, as in the Tufted Titmouse or Ruby-crowned Kinglet. An eye stripe or line is a dark line that runs through the eye. A superciliary eye stripe is a dark or light stripe or line that runs above the eye, rather like an eyebrow. The Carolina

The Rose-breasted Grosbeak has a large, conical bill and strong jaw muscles well adapted to cracking open seeds.

The Tufted Titmouse, a common backyard bird, has a big-eyed look because the black eye is circled by a black eye ring. This bird also has a short crest, or tuft, on its head.

Wren and the Chipping Sparrow, for example, have conspicuous white eye stripes.

Eye color is sometimes an important field mark, but it is a difficult one to see. Despite its name, the Red-eyed Vireo is much more easily identified by other field marks, such as its monotonously repeated call, its conspicuous white superciliary eye stripe, and its blue-gray cap. The Brown Thrasher has yellowish eyes, but you should easily be able to identify this bird from other, more obvious field marks, such as its long, cinnamon-colored tail.

Head markings, such as the bright chestnut cap on the Chipping Sparrow, are good, easily visible field marks.

The color of the lores (the area between the base of the upper mandible and the eyes) is sometimes given as a field mark. If the bird has an eye ring and lores of the same color and also has a dark eye stripe, it may be described as wearing spectacles. Many vireos have this characteristic field mark.

Head markings such as stripes can easily be seen on birds such as White-crowned Sparrows. Colored caps or crowns are good field marks, as in the Black-capped Chickadee. The Chipping Sparrow can be spotted at a distance by its rusty cap; this is also a good field mark for the Palm Warbler. Look for crests or other unusual formations on the head. Crests are seen on such birds as cardinals, Tufted Titmice, Cedar Waxwings, and Pileated Woodpeckers ("pileated" means "crowned" or "crested"). Some ducks have large crests. Good examples are the Wood Duck and many sea ducks such as Buffleheads and Goldeneyes. Horned Larks have little "horns" on top of the head behind the eyes (these can be hard to see).

Face masks are easily seen on Cedar Waxwings and Common Yellowthroats. As their name suggests, hoods can be seen on the Hooded Warbler and Hooded Oriole, as well as the Connecticut Warbler and other birds.

Throat and breast

If you can get a glimpse of a bird's throat and breast, look for patches of color at the throat and for the presence or absence of stripes and streaks on the breast. Throat patches are conspicuous field marks for such birds as the White-throated Sparrow and the Ruby-throated Hummingbird. Throat patches are also good clues when identifying some warblers: The Blackburnian Warbler has a distinctive orange throat patch.

Stripes, streaks, and spots on the breast, or the lack thereof, are useful field marks. Many thrushes, for example, have streaked breasts. The presence or absence of streaks and spots is also helpful when identifying sparrows.

Wings

After getting a good look at the head, move on to the wings and look for bars and patches. These are usually thin lines (bars) or solid patches of a lighter color that run across the folded wings.

The presence (or absence) and number of bars and patches are frequently cited as important field marks. Patches on the underwing, such as those of the Northern Mockingbird, are easily seen when the bird flies.

Wing stripes are lighter- or darker-colored margins along the wing feathers. These are usually not visible when the wings are folded but are quite conspicuous when the bird flies. Wing stripes are particularly helpful for identifying shorebirds such as sandpipers and other waders in flight. It's hard to distinguish the Willet from other marsh sandpipers when they are standing. In flight, however, the Willet shows a prominent white wing stripe. Sometimes the wing is a contrasting color, as in the Scarlet Tanager or Blue-winged Warbler. The color of the wing lining can also be a field mark, especially when viewing the bird in flight from underneath.

Note the shape and length of the folded wing. Swallows, for example, have long, pointed wings that extend almost to the end of the tail when the birds are perched.

It is important to understand the terminology used to describe bird wings because you will encounter these terms often. Study the topographical diagram in your field guide to get a firm grasp on the types of feathers—primaries, secondaries, coverts—and the parts of the wing, especially the leading and trailing edges and the wrist.

Tail

The shape, color, and angle of a bird's tail also provide important identification clues. Note the shape and length of the tail—very long, long, short, stubby, narrow, broad, and so

Members of the wren family are all small and brownish and have upcocked tails held above the body, as in this Carolina Wren. The bright white eye stripe, buffy belly, and stocky shape help distinguish this bird from other wrens.

on—and the shape of its end. Tails can be squared off at the end, notched, pointed, rounded, or deeply forked (as in the Barn Swallow). The position in which the bird holds its tail is also a clue. Some birds, such as wrens, hold their tails cocked up at a jaunty angle; others routinely hold their tails down almost vertically. Some birds, including many flycatchers, "wag" their tails up and down as they perch. The Black-billed Magpie is easily recognized by its very long tail (only a few North American birds have tails longer than their bodies) and white wing patches.

FEET AND LEGS

The color, length, and structure of a bird's feet and legs are sometimes very difficult to see. The feet and legs are not that important for identifying most birds, especially the passerines. However, leg color is helpful for identifying gulls and terns and some shorebirds. Leg length is a good field mark for some wading birds such as sandpipers.

Almost all birds have four toes (a few birds have only three). Webbed or palmated feet are found on swimming birds such as ducks and geese; the webbing is between the three front toes. Birds such as cormorants and pelicans are totipalmate: They have webbing between all four toes. One of the more baffling bird names you will encounter is that of the Semipalmated Sandpiper, one of the most abundant shorebirds. The name describes the bird's feet, which have partial webbing between the toes.

Some birds that swim and walk on land about equally, such as coots and grebes, have lobed, paddle-shaped toes. Birds of prey (raptors) have powerful, clawed toes that are highly separated. Passerines have four separate toes, generally with three facing forward and one facing backward; these feet are designed for perching. Woodpeckers are zygodactylic: They have two toes facing forward and two facing backward. The ptarmigans have "snowshoes" of feathers on their feet to help them walk on the surface of snow.

You won't get many opportunities to use these terms because you probably won't get a very close look at the feet of a wading or swimming bird. Learn the vocabulary so you can sound reasonably intelligent—especially if you can work

Although leg color is an important field mark for shorebirds such as this Greater Yellowlegs, it's also often very hard to see. In part that's because you usually can't get close enough to get a really good look at the legs and in part because the legs may be partially submerged or covered with mud. Look for other field marks, such as the thin neck, long bill (longer than the head), and slender body, to confirm your identification.

"zygodactylic" into the conversation—but don't count on foot structure as a field mark for identification purposes.

Flight

Just when you get your binoculars focused on that brown bird in the branches, off it flies. Don't give up—the flight itself can help you identify the bird. Some field marks are visible only when the bird flies. Indeed, the appearance of the bird in flight is practically the only way to identify some of the look-alike shorebirds. A more familiar example is the Dark-eyed Junco, which is easily spotted by the flashing of its white outer tail feathers as it takes flight.

The way the bird flies is also a clue. Hummingbirds hover, fly backward, and even fly upside down. Dabbling ducks take off from the water in one jump, whereas diving ducks have to patter along the surface building up speed before they can take off. Hawks soar; swallows fly with elegant strength; Northern Mockingbirds fly with very slow wing beats; and woodpeckers have an undulating flight, folding their wings against their bodies after several wing beats. With experience, you will be able to identify many birds simply by the way they fly. This is a skill worth cultivating, if only because it deeply impresses nonbirders.

POSTURE

The way a bird stands, perches, and moves is another helpful clue. Some birds perch with an upright posture, whereas others perch more horizontally. Note also the way the bird walks. Does it hop on both feet? Does it walk on alternate feet?

IDENTIFICATION COMPLICATIONS

Seasonal plumage changes can seriously complicate life for beginning birders. A bird's most vivid and recognizable plumage occurs during the breeding season. When that period is over, the bird's distinctive colors and patterns can gradually fade. This is exemplified by the warblers, whose bright spring colors and clear markings become drab and indistinguishable by autumn. Roger Tory Peterson coined the very apt phrase "confusing fall warblers" to describe the phenomenon.

Shorebird identification is also complicated by seasonal plumage changes. Gull identification is further complicated by seasonal changes and by the plumage changes that immature birds go through before reaching adulthood.

Identification challenges of this sort are extremely interesting for advanced birders and extremely frustrating for beginners. If you can't identify the species, just let it go as an unidentified warbler, sandpiper, or gull.

Making the Identification

The illustrations in your field guide present the birds in static profile wearing idealized plumage. Surprisingly often, birds actually do present themselves in profile and hold still long enough for you to get a good look. Often enough, however, they are far less obliging. As discussed elsewhere, you must apply all your birding techniques to getting a glimpse of a good field mark or a distinctive piece of behavior.

Sometimes all you need is the one definitive field mark that excludes all other possibilities. If you see a small, bright yellow bird with black wings, it can be only an American Goldfinch.

It is more likely that you will have to narrow down the possibilities by a process of elimination. Start by trying to place the bird in its proper family. The good field mark, along with your overall impression of other characteristics, should at least get you into the right section of your field guide. After looking at the descriptions in the most likely family, you can try to pin your bird down specifically. Check the range maps. Birds do stray from where they should be, but the odds are against it. Check the habitat. Again, birds are sometimes found outside their usual habitat but not often.

To take a real-life example, suppose you are birding in a marshy area—Jamaica Bay in New York City—and you notice a small, brownish bird moving restlessly among the phragmites. As the bird briefly pops up into an open space, you distinctly see that its short tail is cocked upward; you get the impression that the bird has a white eye stripe, but it vanishes again before you can be sure. What bird have you seen?

The upcocked tail tells you that the bird is some sort of wren. But which of the nine possible wrens is it? By looking at the range maps, you can immediately eliminate those that are not found on the East Coast. This removes Bewick's Wren, the Cactus Wren, the Rock Wren, and the Canyon Wren from consideration, leaving you with only five possibilities. By considering the habitat, you can further eliminate the House Wren, Winter Wren, and Carolina Wren (probably). Now you are left with just two likely possibilities: Sedge Wren or Marsh Wren. Habitat and the general impression that the bird has a white eye stripe point you directly at Marsh Wren.

The first time you go through this process, you may not find the bird, probably because you are looking in the wrong family. It's very easy to confuse a female Rose-breasted Grosbeak with a member of the sparrow family, for example, and even very experienced birdwatchers can't tell some of the flycatchers apart. Even if you get close on the first try, it could take you a long time to decide on the final identification. The whole laborious business can start to make you feel terribly inept. You will despair of ever achieving the immediate identifications that other birders do with such nonchalant ease. Stay with it. The day will come when, catching sight of an interesting bird, to your own surprise you automatically identify it correctly.

Work at your identifications but don't get hung up on identifying every bird you see, especially if it means that you're not having any fun. Remember the words of Walt Whitman, an enthusiastic if somewhat indiscriminate nature lover: "You must not know too much, or be too precise or scientific about birds and trees and flowers . . . ; a certain free margin, and even vagueness . . . helps your enjoyment of these things."

4

BIRDING BY EAR

When it comes to finding and identifying birds, sound can be as important as appearance. Learning to recognize bird sounds will increase your enjoyment of birding enormously.

Songs and Sounds

Birds make a variety of sounds with a variety of purposes. The most recognizable bird sounds are the lovely notes warbled by songbirds, but virtually all birds (swans and vultures are among the rare exceptions) have songs of a sort and make other sounds called "vocalizations." All bird vocalizations are produced by the syrinx, an organ located in the trachea just above the branching of the bronchi leading to the lungs. As a rule, the more developed the syrinx, the more complex the sounds it can produce. Songbirds generally have highly developed syrinxes and thus produce the most complex songs. Interestingly, because a song is produced entirely within the syrinx, many birds can sing with their mouths full or even closed.

Every songbird species has a distinctly different song, full of rich harmonics. Birds outside the songbird family also produce distinctly different calls and other sounds that are an aid to identifying the species and to determining where the bird is and what it is doing. For example, it is visually difficult to tell the difference between a Lesser and Greater Yellowlegs unless two birds are near each other for a size comparison. However, the voices of the two species are quite different and easily distinguished.

SONGS

Birdsong or vocalization, whether complex or simple, is a male function, designed primarily to define territory. Another significant function is to attract a mate; this accomplished, the male sings to his mate to strengthen the pair bond. (With rare exceptions and despite all the inaccurate poetry about nightingales, most female birds in temperate zones do not sing.) The same functions of birdsong are accomplished in other ways by some other birds. Woodpeckers, for example, define their territories and attract females by drumming on resonant surfaces such as trees (and sometimes houses or even cars). Male Ruffed Grouse display for females by beating their wings, making a noise that sounds almost exactly like a distant motorcycle starting up.

Birdsong reaches its peak in the early mornings of spring, when male birds are vying for territory and advertising for mates. A bird walk through woods and fields at this time of year is a delightful cacophony of sounds. Singing drops off noticeably after the birds get organized, with all the borders staked out and females spoken for, but it continues at a reduced level into the breeding season. By midsummer, birdsong almost ceases.

Singing birds in the spring are easy to find—just follow the sound to the tree branch or shrub that contains the singer. The birds will generally be found perched prominently on the tops of the trees, at the ends of the branches, on fence posts,

Singing birds in the spring, such as this Song Sparrow, are males staking out their territory and hoping to attract a female to it. During this time, males tend to select visible perches, making them easy to find and watch. If the bird notices you, it will probably stop singing and may fly off a short distance. Remain quietly where you are, and the bird will probably pop up and begin to sing again.

or on top of other vegetation or telephone poles, the better to project their voices, keep an eye on the competition, and spot any interested females. Singing birds generally adopt erect postures, with the head back and the beak wide open. They thoughtfully repeat their songs loudly from the same place, allowing birders to home in.

As part of claiming their territory, some birds such as cardinals will countersing or duet with nearby rivals. When this occurs, first one and then the other bird sings alternately. After you realize that at least two birds are involved, you can separate the sounds and go in search of one or the other.

Locating a singing bird can be difficult. The first step is simply to stand still and listen intently, concentrating on only the bird you are tracking. This can be surprisingly difficult, especially for city dwellers who are accustomed to ignoring all the undifferentiated noises constantly around them. It can also be difficult for older birders, who may no longer be able to hear very quiet song or the high notes. Try turning your head slowly from side to side while listening; you should hear the bird more loudly toward one side or the other. All members of a group should listen carefully and slowly point to where they think the sound is coming from. Theoretically, doing this should yield an accurate consensus. There's a good chance, of course, that just when you think you have located the bird, it will fly away. Stick with it. Generally, a territorial bird won't fly far, and you still have a good chance of getting a look at it. If the bird flew because you disturbed it, wait quietly until it settles down again. Singing will probably resume soon.

In general, birds sing the most in the early morning and toward dusk. Some birds, including some flycatchers and swallows, sing special dawn songs just before day breaks. The function of dawn songs, aside from their beauty, is unclear, unless they are an incentive to birdwatchers to get up early.

OTHER SOUNDS

Particularly among songbirds, a distinction is generally made between songs and other sounds. Male, female, and young birds all produce a wide range of calls and other sounds that helps the birder locate and identify them. Generally, a bird's repertory of sounds falls into several convenient categories: alarm calls, contact calls, flocking calls, feeding calls, begging calls, flight calls, aggressive calls, and nonvocal sounds such as woodpecker drumming and the whirring wing sound that Mourning Doves make when they take flight. Unfortunately, these sounds are often not as well defined as songs, making it difficult sometimes to determine which bird is making the sound and why.

Especially to inexperienced birders, the various chips and chirps made by different birds sound much alike. With practice, you will gradually begin to recognize the more obvious differences among species. Some differences are so slight as to be virtually undetectable; in such cases, even experienced birders need other clues to identify the bird.

What a particular bird sound means must often be determined from the context. For example, the contact call (the sound that members of a pair make to keep in touch with each other) of the White-breasted Nuthatch is often described as *yank* or *yank-yank*. The same call, given louder and more frequently, is an alarm call.

Learning Bird Sounds

A unique sort of vocabulary is used by the authors of field guides and other written descriptions to transcribe bird sounds. When you read descriptions, the easiest to remember and imagine are those that are onomatopoeic, or imitative of the actual sound. A classic example is the *chicka-dee-dee-dee* call of the Black-capped Chickadee, which sounds exactly as it is written. Other songs and calls are not as easy. Songs are often described as melodious, clear, whistled, and slurred. Calls may be described as a harsh chatter, buzzy trill, or rattle. Songs and calls are also often transliterated as a burry *teeooo*, raspy *chur*, or a simple *chip, tseep*, or even *ik* or *chjjj*. Even worse from a beginner's standpoint are descriptions that compare one bird's song with another's because you are likely to be unfamiliar with both. And what exactly is the difference between sounds that are buzzy, burry, and raspy?

Beginning birders can take comfort in the knowledge that the experts disagree among themselves about how to describe and transliterate bird sounds. For example, Roger Tory Peterson renders the song of the Acadian Flycatcher as "a sharp explosive *pit-see*," whereas other guides render it variously as *PEET-sah, peet-suh,* and *flee-see*; the usual mnemonic is *Pizza!* or *Free beer!* (The mnemonic for the closely related Olive-sided Flycatcher is usually rendered as *Quick! Three beers.*)

No amount of puzzling over the correct pronunciation of *tsickajwee-jwee* (Tufted Titmouse) or *woika woika* (Red-bellied Woodpecker) can ever substitute for hearing the real thing. Ideally you will locate and identify a new bird, hear it vocalize, and forever remember the sound and associate it with a clear mental image of the bird. The association can be complicated by some variables. Many songbirds sing individual variations on the basic song, and individual birds sing variations of their variations. Some birds do good imitations of other birds— Blue Jays often imitate the screams of hawks, and the Nothern Mockingbird's song consists of nothing but imitations of other birds. In addition, the basic song can vary by geography. In effect, birds develop dialects. This is often noted even by casual birdwatchers when they hear song sparrows in other parts of the country. Finally, birds make lots of simple call noises that sound a lot like those of other birds. Remember that even the most experienced birders usually know only the usual territorial song and most common call sounds for a species. When all you hear are assorted *chips,* you might as well give up on an aural identification. Use the sounds to locate the bird for a visual identification instead.

Sonograms

Some field guides provide a sonogram, or visual representation of the song, by the description of the bird. At first glance, sonograms seem arcane and impenetrable. They are, in fact, more useful after you are familiar with the bird's song, but they provide helpful information even if you're not after you know how to read them. The vertical axis of a sonogram indicates the pitch (frequency) of the song, as measured in hertz (Hz) or kilohertz (kHz—one kilohertz is the equivalent of 1,000 hertz). For a reference point, middle C on a piano is at 0.262 kHz; the highest C on a piano is at 4.186 kHz. Most birdsongs take place between 2 and 6 kHz (2,000 and 6,000 hertz), with much of them above 4 kHz. Older birders may no longer be able to hear birdsong at pitches above 6 kHz. The horizontal axis of a sonogram indicates the duration of the song; most sonograms are given in 2.5-second segments. The louder the sound, the darker the marks. Thus, the hieroglyphic dark markings within the sonogram indicate the pitch, duration, and loudness of the various notes in the song.

By looking at a sonogram, you can get a good idea of the general nature of a particular bird's song. The higher the frequency in kHz, the higher pitched the sound. The more clearly defined the frequency, the purer the sound and the fewer harmonic overtones it has. Clear whistles appear as thin bands within a narrow frequency range; buzzy trills are thick bands within a wide frequency range. Repeated elements can easily be seen.

A good way to begin understanding sonograms is to study that of the Wood Thrush. This common woodland bird has an easily learned, distinctive, and very beautiful song that begins with high, flutelike notes and ends in a soft trill. The range in kHz is from just below 2 up to nearly 8; the song lasts for about 2.5 seconds and is generally repeated ten to twenty times in a minute. Look at the sonogram while listening to the song to see how the sound relates to the visual representation. The loud, clear notes in the first part of the song are shown by thin, dark bands, whereas the trill in the last part is shown by a much thicker band that has two parts: a heavy band ranging from about 5 kHz to nearly 8 kHz and a series of vertical bands underneath it ranging from 2 to about 4.5 kHz that represents the harmonic tones of the trill. Pay careful attention to the duration of the song and how often it is repeated—these are very helpful identification clues.

Mnemonics

After you've actually heard a song, a mnemonic that attempts to capture its rhythm and cadence helps you remember and identify the song the next time. A mnemonic by definition is memorable. After you've learned a mnemonic like "When I see one I shall seize one and I'll squeeze it 'til it SQUIRTS!" for the Warbling Vireo, it's hard to forget. Simpler examples of birdsong mnemonics include "Potato chip, potato chip" for the American Goldfinch and "Cheerily, cheerily, cheer up" for the American Robin. There's disagreement about some mnemonics. The White-throated Sparrow says "Poor Sam Peabody, Peabody, Peabody" if you're a Yankee and "Sweet sweet Canada, Canada, Canada" if you're not. (Roger Tory Peterson steers clear of controversy by describing the song of this bird as "several clear pensive whistles.") Birds don't necessarily start their songs at the "beginning." They sometimes begin in the middle of a phrase or add a note or two before getting down to the real song. The American Goldfinch, for example, often says "Chip, potato chip, potato chip."

Birdsong Recordings

The next-best learning activity to seeing and hearing a singing bird is listening to recordings. Many birdsong CDs and DVDs are now available. Some briefly present the most characteristic songs or sounds of the birds in strict taxonomic order, with a human voice stating the bird name before the sound. Others are keyed to the most common field guides, making it easier to find the recording of a particular bird.

Taxonomic recordings are useful as reference tools—for verifying your identification of a particular bird—but they are not very helpful for learning the sounds to begin with. A better choice is recordings that take a teaching approach, including explanatory narrations and accompanying booklets or books.

These recordings cover the common species not taxonomically but rather holistically. Some group the birds by similar or related sounds, using the compare-and-contrast method. Others focus on a particular group of birds such as owls or warblers or on birds of a particular habitat such as common backyard birds or shorebirds or on birds of a region. These recordings also present many or all of the sounds that a particular species makes, not just its song or most common sound. The two volumes of *Know Your Bird Sounds,* by renowned field recorder Lang Elliott, are an excellent starting point for beginners. Other recordings are also good choices: The Peterson field guide series offers a number of choices, and the Stokes guides to eastern and western birds are popular. Digitized versions can be loaded onto an iPod or iPhone. The BirdJam iPhone/iPod application, based on the Stokes field guide CDs, provides multiple sounds and photos for over nine hundred North American birds. Additional modules break out bird songs into categories, such as eastern warblers.

The *Backyard Birdsong Guide* by Donald Kroodsma, available in eastern and western editions, contains a built-in push-button audio player. These volumes are good home study tools.

Handheld dedicated birdsong devices are a good learning tool that can also be carried easily into the field. National Geographic offers Handheld Birds, based on the National Geographic field guide and including sound from the Cornell Laboratory of Ornithology. The IdentiFlyer is an identification tool that uses an optical scanner in a handheld wand to read a bar code next to a picture of a bird in the accompanying booklet. The wand then plays the bird song.

Bird sounds are often very similar to other sounds in nature. The indignant squeak of a startled chipmunk, for example, can sound very much like the noise made by a startled towhee. Because both noises will come from the underbrush in a wooded area, you could easily start looking for a bird that isn't there or decide not to look for one that is. Alternatively, you might decide that the trilling noise coming from an overgrown field is an insect when, in fact, it is coming from the aptly named Grasshopper Sparrow. The more inexperienced you are, the harder it is to distinguish between bird sounds and those made by insects, frogs, squirrels, and other creatures. Recordings of the sound of a particular habitat such as a wetlands region can help you learn the differences.

Many birders listen to recordings while driving, but you should probably be alone or in the company of a fellow enthusiast if you do this. These are not the sort of CDs your carpool will necessarily appreciate, especially if you like to practice your bird imitations while listening. Dozing pets will often awaken when you play the recording; they may then proceed to bark at or look for the "bird." This response can be deafening when dogs are passengers in the car. Fortunately, all cats and all but the most obtuse dogs quickly realize that there is no bird and that it is safe to go back to sleep.

For many people, the best way to listen to bird recordings is to listen for only ten minutes or so but to listen often. Some people have a natural ability—sometimes but not always correlated with musical talent—for learning bird sounds quickly. Most beginners need a fair amount of repetition.

SMART BIRDING

A very portable, inexpensive, simple device that would instantly show a picture and play the birdsong you need for identification was once only a dream for birders. No longer. Highly sophisticated yet easy-to-use birding applications for the iPhone, iPod, and similar devices make it possible to find and play a birdsong in seconds while looking at a picture. BirdJam, one of the most popular apps, organizes bird songs into natural groupings, such as ducks or warblers, and allows searching by name, habitat, bird family, or taxonomic order. You can also upload any birdsong CD or recording from your personal collection.

Digital field guides are also now available for smart devices. The National Geographic Handheld Birds device can also be put onto an iPhone or iPod; the Peterson field guide has a digital version, and iBird Explorer, available in several versions, is an excellent and very versatile field guide application. The future of birding is digital and portable; expect many developments.

Bird Videos

Videos featuring birds are useful and enjoyable tools for learning to identify birds both visually and aurally. A wide selection of longer nature videos, such as the outstanding series *The Life of Birds* featuring David Attenborough, is available through Netflix under the category of science and nature documentaries; you may be able to order some of these DVDs through your public library. More entertaining in their own way are the many shorter clips of birds that are posted on online shared video sites such as YouTube. The quality of these videos can vary widely, from blurry clips with no sound to very professional clips with excellent production values. Search for any bird of interest, and at least half a dozen clips are likely to come up. This is a great way to fill in a few idle or work-avoiding minutes—the information from a short video featuring a single bird species is likely to stick with you.

5

BIRD BEHAVIOR

When you observe bird behavior, you realize that there is no such thing as an uninteresting bird. Behavior watching adds depth and insight to your birding as well as giving you valuable clues that help you identify and appreciate the bird.

FEEDING BEHAVIOR

Birds spend a lot of time looking for food, which means that birdwatchers spend a lot of time watching them do it. How a bird finds its food, what it eats, and how it consumes it are valuable identification clues. A bird's feeding strategy can help you identify it by family and by species.

Overall, birds consume an amazing variety of food, much of it unpalatable by human standards. Earthworms, carrion, spiders, tadpoles, poison ivy berries, and grass are just some of the foods eaten by various birds. Some birds, such as Snail Kites, have very specific dietary preferences, whereas others, such as crows, will eat almost anything.

To find their food, birds employ a number of feeding strategies. Many strategies are common or even unique to a particular bird family; however, many birds employ more than one feeding strategy or employ a particular strategy only when a particular food is abundant. By observing the feeding strategy of a mystery bird, you can probably place it into the correct family and then move on to identify the species.

PECKING

Probably the most familiar feeding behavior is pecking, in which the bird searches on the ground for food, picking up seeds, insects, and other food. This is very common behavior for passerines such as sparrows, juncos, finches, and Mourning Doves, and for larger gallinaceous (chicken-like) birds such as Ruffed Grouse, Northern Bobwhite, and Wild Turkey.

Often the bird scratches at the ground or uses both feet to stir up the leaf litter and reveal insects, seeds, and nuts. Pecking and leaf tossing can be seen easily in your backyard under the birdfeeder by watching the juncos, House Sparrows, and White-throated Sparrows. You will also often see Fox Sparrows and towhees doing this. On a bird walk, listen for the rustling noises these birds make as they forage. Pecking birds tend to be found on or near the ground, often in open areas such as fields, roadsides, yards, and open woods.

PROBING

Of all the familiar bird feeding behaviors, probing may be the most familiar of all because it is performed by that most familiar of birds, the American Robin. When you watch this bird take a few steps across the lawn, pause, cock its head, and then suddenly thrust its bill down into the ground and come up with a worm, you are seeing the probing strategy in action. (Despite the appearance of listening, American Robins actually cock their heads to focus the fovea—the most sensitive part of the eye—on the ground to spot the movement of the worm. In general, birds don't have particularly acute hearing.)

Numerous shorebirds, including dowitchers, godwits, sandpipers, and others, probe the sand and mud for food. Dowitchers and godwits probe with a characteristic rapid "sewing-machine" movement. American Woodcocks and Common Snipe also probe for food.

"Probing" also refers to poking into and under bark and other cracks and crevices to find food. Among the common backyard birds, Brown Creepers and nuthatches are champion probers.

CHISELING

Woodpeckers are the clearest example of chiseling as a feeding strategy. Chiseling works in two ways: First, the pounding on a tree trunk makes a hole and exposes the insects, insect eggs, and larvae; second, the pounding disturbs other insects and makes them come to the surface, where they are promptly eaten. The noise made by a foraging woodpecker is easily heard in the woods but can be hard to pinpoint because it is irregular. Look for large trees with dead portions, dead or dying trees, or trees with old broken branches and stubs; these tend to have insects boring into them and are attractive to woodpeckers. Even if you don't actually see the woodpecker, you can see signs of its activity: fresh holes in the tree and wood chips on the ground. Look at the size and shape of the hole. Pileated Woodpeckers make large, oblong holes; Hairy and Downy Woodpeckers make smaller, rounded holes.

Sapsuckers use another form of chiseling to drill rows of small holes, or wells, in the bark of trees. The sapsuckers use

To excavate a nesting hole, this Red-headed Woodpecker has braced himself with his strong tail feathers and is using his chisel-shaped bill to make the chips fly.

their brushlike tongue to lick up the sap that accumulates. If you find a tree with sapsucker wells, sit down and watch it for a while. Other birds, including hummingbirds, warblers, and vireos, may visit the spot to feed on the nectar and the insects it attracts.

Woodpeckers are often unfairly accused of killing trees. There is some slight truth to this accusation because sapsuckers (small North American woodpeckers) occasionally drill their holes so efficiently that they girdle the tree, and it eventually dies. Usually, however, the tree is already dying from insect infestation, which is what attracts the woodpeckers to begin with.

PERCH-GLEANING

The strategy of searching for insects and other small prey such as spiders or insect eggs while perched on a branch or twig is called "perch-gleaning." Warblers, which eat insects almost exclusively, use this strategy frequently as they move through the woods and underbrush. Perch-gleaning birds usually move rapidly and energetically in their search for food. They will land on a branch, search the immediate area, and then flit on to another nearby spot. This activity is one way to distinguish between warblers and other, slower-moving denizens of the treetops such as vireos.

You can easily observe perch-gleaning by watching chickadees and titmice forage. These energetic, acrobatic little birds search rapidly among bark, leaves, and other foliage, sometimes hanging upside down, and then move quickly to another spot. Perch-gleaning behavior is seen even when these birds take seeds from a feeder: They seize the seeds and dart away to hammer them open and eat them elsewhere.

Plucking and pruning

Many birds eat seeds and fruits that they pluck or glean directly from the vegetation. For example, Cedar Waxwings love to eat berries, wild cherries, and grapes. Members of a small flock of these birds will descend on a wild cherry tree and eat their fill, sometimes politely passing the fruits to each other. Goldfinches land on the seed heads of wild grasses and glean the seeds, along with any insects they find. Other birds that eat seeds and fruit in this manner include Purple Finches, House Finches, and Blue Jays. An excellent way to observe this

Cedar Waxwings love to eat berries and small fruit such as cherries. Small flocks often descend on bushes or trees and feed for hours. The bonanza for the birds is also one for birders. The birds are usually so intent on the food that they can be easily watched from a fairly close distance.

feeding strategy is to stake out a food source such as a patch of ripe berries and wait to see which birds come to exploit it.

Pruning is a more specialized feeding strategy. Birds such as grosbeaks and Ruffed Grouse nip off the tender, nutritious buds of trees and plants.

HAWKING

The hawking approach is easily seen in the behavior of members of the flycatcher family. The bird perches quietly, often wagging its tail slowly up and down, then suddenly darts out, seizes a passing insect, and returns to its original perch or another one nearby. Phoebes and other flycatchers often find telephone wires or branches on the edges of open areas or ponds to be convenient hawking sites. Kingbirds prefer bushes in open fields. Some flycatchers, including the Willow, Least, and Acadian, dart out to capture insects that are on leaves or branches, a form of hawking sometimes called "sally-gleaning." You might also spot a Red-eyed Vireo sally gleaning. Birds that are not part of the flycatcher family also hawk for insects. The list includes Cedar Waxwings and some woodpeckers.

ON THE WING

Some insect-eating birds such as swallows, swifts, and nighthawks capture their prey in flight. The graceful gyrations of swallows as they pursue insects on the wing are a birder's delight. An interesting feature of all these birds is their wide gape—that is, the soft, fleshy tissue around the corners of the mouth. The wide gape in effect makes their mouths bigger, allowing the birds to engulf their insect prey easily.

Barn Swallows are very common and easy to watch; other swallows, such as Tree Swallows, are also quite common. Look for them perched on telephone wires, especially in areas near open fields and lakes.

RAPTOR FEEDING

Birds of prey generally capture their meals by seizing them after a pursuit (accipiters such as Cooper's Hawks, for example) or by pouncing on them from above (owls, eagles, and buteos such as Red-tailed Hawks, for example). Peregrines and other falcons capture their prey by stooping—diving down on the prey at great speed. Kestrels and Rough-legged Hawks hover hunt, beating their wings rapidly to hold themselves stationary in the air before pouncing.

The short, rounded wings and long tails of the accipiters are superb adaptations for chasing small birds through wooded areas. Watching a Sharp-shinned Hawk pursue a bird while it twists among the tree trunks with incredible speed and agility is a sight that will take your breath away the first time you see it. If you visit a hawkwatching locale during the autumn or spring migration, it is a sight you have a reasonably good chance of seeing. Accipiters sometimes pick off birds at feeders. This is perfectly natural; don't interfere. Think of it as another type of bird feeding.

Red-tailed Hawks and the other buteos such as the Broad-winged Hawk are heavier and larger than the accipiters. Their prey is usually larger as well: Rodents and rabbits are preferred. Buteos soar in high, lazy circles, watching the ground for unwary prey. They then drop down rapidly in a steep dive and land, feet first, on the prey. Red-tailed Hawks are the most common and widespread hawk in North America. Although there is a fair amount of variation, Red-tails are basically easy to spot and identify as they circle; look for the characteristic rusty-colored tail. If a Red-tail wants a closer look at a possible meal, it may face into the wind and hold itself motionless, an action known as "kiting" for its resemblance to a kite on a string. Red-tailed Hawks often drift out of sight before you get a chance to see them kite or dive.

The hover-hunting and pouncing behavior of American Kestrels can be seen without difficulty. These handsome little hawks are quite common. Look for them on telephone wires and poles, fence posts, and other lookout perches near open areas such as fields or even highway median strips. When a kestrel spots something to eat, such as a small rodent or a grasshopper, it may pounce immediately. Alternatively, kestrels cruise their territory, hover when they spot potential prey, and then pounce.

The chances of your seeing one of nature's most dramatic moments—a Peregrine Falcon stooping on its prey—are much better than they once were. Thanks to successful release programs across North America, these endangered birds now live comfortably atop tall buildings and bridges in cities such as Cincinnati, Calgary, Baltimore, Los Angeles, New York, San Diego, Winnipeg, and Pittsburgh. You may also be fortunate enough to see a Peregrine fly past a hawkwatching site during the autumn migration. If you are extremely fortunate and have fast reflexes, you may see it stoop.

Scavenging

Vultures, crows, and gulls are nature's clean-up crew. These birds spot dead animals from the air, then land and feed on them. Vultures eat almost nothing but carrion; crows and gulls are much more flexible. Turkey Vultures and Black Vultures are often seen soaring slowly over their large territories. You can usually watch them turn their heads slowly from side to side, looking for carcasses as they soar. If you notice several vultures making low, tight circles, chances are something large and dead, like a deer, is below them somewhere. You may also startle a vulture dining on road kill by the side of a quiet country road.

Plunging

When you are birdwatching in a marshy area, you may see a dark, chunky shape hover briefly over some water, then suddenly drop down into it head first. Before the splash is over, the bird flies back up, usually with a small fish in its mouth, and lands on an overhanging branch. You have just seen a Belted Kingfisher plunging for prey. Plunging birds dive all the way into the water from the air or from a perch. Other plunging birds include pelicans, ospreys, and terns—all fish-eaters. White Pelicans are quite common along the West and Gulf coasts; Brown Pelicans are less common but perhaps more familiar, especially to visitors to Florida, because they often hang around fishing piers looking for handouts. Despite their awkwardness on land, pelicans are marvelous flyers. You have a pretty good chance of seeing them if you visit an ocean coast or take a sea-going boat trip.

That terns generally plunge into the water in pursuit of food on or just below the surface is one good way to distinguish them from gulls. As with pelicans, your best chance of seeing this behavior is to look in coastal areas or offshore.

GRAZING

Geese, including the very familiar Canada Goose, graze on vegetation on the land or water's edge by pulling it up or biting it off. Any large bird that seems to be nibbling the ground is a goose.

DABBLING

One of birding's more endearing moments is watching a dabbling duck such as a mallard up-end itself and waggle its rump

How a waterbird floats is a clue to its identity. Birds such as loons, grebes, and cormorants float low in the water, often appearing to be partially submerged, with their tails underwater, as with this Common Loon.

Ducks, such as this male Wood Duck in full breeding plumage, float high in the water, with their tails generally well above the surface.

while feeding underwater. More practically, feeding behavior is a good way to narrow down the identity of an unknown duck. Dabbling or surface-feeding ducks are usually found in shallow areas of salt- and freshwater marshes or on other shallow water such as small ponds. This is because they feed by eating vegetable matter on or just below the surface. Mallards, Black Ducks, Pintails, Blue-winged Teal, and other dabbling ducks often share their habitat, especially during migration periods, with bay ducks such as Redheads and Canvasbacks and sea ducks such as Buffleheads and Common Goldeneyes. The differences in feeding behavior can help you sort out the different species.

The feathers of cormorants and the Anhinga become saturated with water when they dive; this probably reduces the birds' buoyancy and lets them submerge more easily. When they surface, they hang out their wings to dry. This handsome Anhinga in the Florida Everglades is drying its wings and also warming its body.

DIVING

Diving birds float on the water's surface and then submerge completely in pursuit of prey or vegetable matter. Bay ducks and sea ducks commonly dive for their food. If you are watching a duck, and it tips itself up and disappears under water, it is a diving duck. Other diving birds include mergansers, grebes, cormorants, and Anhinga. Grebes dive by silently sinking out of sight, a slightly unnerving thing to watch.

As a rule, swimming and diving birds are well adapted to a watery life, with feathers that shed water. Cormorants and Anhingas, however, are not waterproof. After diving for food, they must spread their wings out to dry in the sun. Cormorants and Anhingas are thus very easy to spot on land. In coastal wetlands, look for large, blackish birds perched on pilings, tree stubs, and the like, with their wings held half open. Double-crested Cormorants are widespread, even inland; Anhingas are found in freshwater swampy areas in Florida and along the Gulf Coast.

STALKING

Many members of the heron family stand in or wade through shallow water in search of live prey, a strategy known as "stalking." A stalking Great Blue Heron clarifies the Zenlike connection between stillness and motion. The bird stands for long moments in shallow water, motionless but deeply intent, then darts with lightning speed and unerring accuracy to snatch its prey from the water. Great Blue Herons are the largest herons in North America. They are common and easy to watch in both salt- and freshwater wetlands. These herons are surprisingly tolerant of humans. They will often let you get quite close and will sometimes even accept handouts.

Canopy feeding is a refinement of the stalking strategy. Some herons, including Reddish Egrets and Snowy Egrets, stand in shallow water with their wings spread up and outward. Exactly why the birds do this is not really understood. Many researchers believe that the outspread wings act as a sunshade, blocking glare on the water and giving the bird a better view of possible prey.

Sediment stirring

Shorebirds and wading birds that feed on small organisms sometimes stir up the sediment in shallow water to find their prey. Herons, egrets, and storks all do this. A good example is the way the Snowy Egret delicately dabbles shallow water with its yellow feet as it flies past. Another approach to sediment stirring is followed by phalaropes, which spin in circles like tops in shallow water to stir up food with their lobed feet.

Surface feeding

Gulls and many other sea birds such as petrels and shearwaters obtain their food by plucking it from the water's surface. Indeed, the name "shearwater" comes from the way these birds fly just along the very edge of waves; sometimes the wingtips of shearwaters can be seen actually dipping into the water as the birds fly. With consummate skill, these birds pluck fish, shrimp, and other food from the water. You can easily watch a Herring Gull surface feed by tossing any sort of food—a French fry, for instance—into the water.

Black Skimmers are perhaps the ultimate surface feeders. These intriguing birds fly just above the surface of coastal bays with the long lower mandible of their large red bills shearing through the water. In no other North American bird is the lower mandible longer than the upper; no other bird behaves like a Black Skimmer. Look for flocks of skimmers flying in parallel lines along calm water, especially at dawn and dusk.

PIRACY

If you still have any lingering ideas about innocence in nature, piracy as a feeding strategy will dispel them. Some birds habitually obtain their food by stealing it from other birds. Many gulls are occasional pirates, chasing other birds with food until they drop it. If you watch enough gulls, you will see this happen fairly often. The most skillful pirate is the appropriately named "Parasitic Jaeger." This offshore bird feeds almost exclusively by chasing terns and forcing them to give up their prey. You have a reasonably good chance of seeing this behavior if you take a pelagic birding trip.

HOARDING

Some birds, notably some members of the woodpecker, nuthatch, and jay families, hoard or cache food. Acorn Woodpeckers cram huge numbers of acorns into holes excavated in trees (and also telephone poles, house siding, and anywhere else they can drill a hole). More than 50,000 acorns have been counted in one hoard, or granary. Similar behavior is seen in the Lewis's Woodpecker. The hoarding behavior of the Clark's Nutcracker has been extensively studied. This bird, found in mountainous conifer forests in the western states, stores acorns, nuts, and other food in a variety of places, including in the ground and under leaf litter. It has an amazing ability to find its hoarded food again. If nuthatches come to your backyard feeder, you may see one wedge a sunflower seed under a piece of loose bark or into a crevice in a tree, or you may see it rediscover food stored earlier.

FEEDING FLOCKS

Anyone with a backyard birdfeeder is familiar with feeding flocks. Particularly in winter, birds such as chickadees, titmice, and Downy Woodpeckers form small, mixed flocks and forage together for food. Why is this advantageous? Mixed flocks are more efficient. By flocking together, the birds increase the chances of coming across a good food source (like your feeder), of avoiding areas that have already been picked over, and of overwhelming the defenses of any individual bird that might object to their presence. And because each species in the flock has a slightly different feeding strategy but essentially the same diet, competition for food is reduced relative to the level that would prevail in a same-species flock of the same size. Always look carefully at any flock of feeding birds. You may well see several species.

COMMENSAL FEEDING

Also called "secondary feeding," commensal feeding occurs when one species finds food as a result of another's activity. As mentioned earlier, a good example of this is the way humming-birds and warblers sometimes feed at the holes made by sapsuckers. Among shorebirds, commensal feeding can be seen in "beaters" and "attendants." For example, cormorants often act as beater birds by stirring up prey; they are followed by attendant birds such as Snowy Egrets that snatch up the prey dislodged by the cormorants' feeding activity. Similarly, Cattle Egrets get their name because they follow cows and other livestock, catching the insects these animals stir up with their hooves. Human activity can also be the beater. Birds such as

American Robins and gulls follow tractors in fields to feed on the earthworms and other prey turned up by the plow. Commensal feeding is actually fairly common. After you know what to look for, you will see it often.

Flight Behavior

Birds in flight fill us with longing and admiration. This aspect of birdwatching is endlessly fascinating in itself and is also a big help in answering identification questions.

How birds fly

Basically, a bird's wing is an airfoil. As the bird moves horizontally through the air by flapping its wings, the leading edge of the wing "splits" the air. This makes the air flowing over the top of the wing travel a longer distance than the air flowing under the bottom of the wing. The air flowing over the top of the wing moves faster and thus exerts less pressure (Bernoulli's law, from introductory physics class). The higher pressure underneath the wing forces it up, providing lift. When lift is equal to or greater than the bird's weight, the bird flies. (The aerodynamics of bird flight are extremely interesting but far too complex for this book. For an excellent study of the subject, see *Birds in Flight: The Art and Science of How Birds Fly* by Carrol L. Henderson.)

For observing bird flight, you need to understand the structure of a bird's wing and the function of the primary and secondary feathers. Study the diagram in the front of your field guide to learn about the wing. Primary feathers are the outermost feathers—the ones toward the outer end of the wing.

These are the feathers most responsible for forward thrust and lift. The secondary feathers on the inner part of the wing form a smooth airfoil.

WING SHAPE

Although wing shapes vary enormously among species, all basically function to provide lift for flight. The shape of the wing can help you identify the bird, at least by family. For birds in flight, look for the overall shape of the wing. Does it taper to a point? Is it rounded? Is it narrow or broad? Are the wings long or short in comparison with the body? Can you see slots between the primary feathers at the tip of the wing? Generally, passerines and woodpeckers have wings that taper to a point—as in swallows, for example. Gallinaceous birds such as Wild Turkeys have shorter, rounded wings. Herons have broad, rounded wings, whereas gulls have long, narrow, pointy wings. Crows and vultures have easily visible wing slots.

The shape of a bird's wings (technically, the aspect ratio) indicates the way the bird flies. Gulls, albatrosses, and similar birds have long, narrow wings with a high aspect ratio designed for high-speed gliding. The soft, rounded wings of birds such as quail and grouse have a low aspect ratio that allows fast takeoffs and quick maneuverability. Many birds found in open areas—terns, swallows, kestrels, for example—have wings with pointed tips. These wings are very efficient with little drag, allowing rapid flight in open areas but relatively little maneuverability. Wings designed for soaring have slots between the primary feathers at the wingtips. Air is forced upward through the slots, improving lift and helping birds such as Red-tailed Hawks and Turkey Vultures to soar for hours with little effort.

If you watch different birds in flight, you will soon realize that they fly in different ways. The things to look for here are the bird's body position in flight, the speed of the flight, how the bird moves its wings, and the nature of the flight. Study the illustrations and flight silhouettes in your field guide. Look at the position of the head relative to the wings: Is it above the wings or level with them? Swans, for instance, fly with their necks extended, whereas loons fly with their heads lower than their bodies. Are the bird's feet visible beyond the tail? Next, get an impression of the way the bird flies. Consider its speed and the nature of the wingbeats. Rapid flight is a good field clue, especially when applied relatively—Common Goldeneyes, for example, are very fast fliers, faster than most other sea ducks.

Generally, wingbeats are described in field guides by their amplitude: either shallow or deep (if the guide doesn't mention them, assume that they are not especially noticeable). Green Herons, for instance, fly rapidly with deep wingbeats; geese fly with deep, powerful wingbeats. The flight pattern and rhythm are also clues. Woodpeckers and finches have an undulating flight pattern, as if they were on a roller-coaster; Common Snipe fly in zigzags. Observe the rhythm and wingbeat frequency of the flight. Does the bird flap its wings continuously? Does it flap several times and then glide? If so, count the flaps and try to time the length of the glide. Noting the rhythm of the flight is particularly helpful for identifying flying hawks.

Takeoff

The way a bird takes off helps you determine its identity. This trait is particularly helpful for identifying ducks and other waterfowl. Dabbling ducks such as mallards and Wood Ducks have a larger wing area-to-weight ratio (wing loading) and can take off by springing directly from the water's surface. Diving ducks such as Canvasbacks and Buffleheads have smaller wings relative to their weight and need a running start to get airborne. They head into the wind and patter over the surface to take off. Other waterfowl such as grebes, swans, and geese also need a running start. This is why often only dabblers are found on small bodies of water—they can take off without needing a runway. Divers who land in small ponds sometimes have trouble getting up enough headway to take off. They may be trapped until there's a strong wind.

Flight sounds

Flying birds sometimes make characteristic sounds. To take an obvious example, hummingbirds' wings make a loud humming or whirring sound. Mourning Doves make a whistling noise with their wings. Owls, on the other hand, fly silently. (Wing noises as part of courtship displays are discussed later.) Many birds call in flight. A few, such as the Lark Bunting, sing in flight as well. Birds also call during migration, especially at night. The sounds of geese and ducks can be easily heard on a quiet night. The sounds of migrating passerines are much more difficult or impossible to hear. An interesting area of current research is migration patterns, which are studied using sensitive microphones to record the sounds of migrating birds overhead at night. The recordings are analyzed with computer software to assess which birds flew by and in what numbers.

FLOCKING FLIGHT

The V formation of Canada Geese in flight is well known to almost everyone. Look carefully at any V formation: It is probably geese, but it could be ducks, swans, cormorants, or Glossy Ibis. Listen while you watch. Canada Geese are extremely noisy in flight, honking constantly, whereas the other birds are quieter; cormorants are silent. Migrating ducks and swans often fly in lines instead of Vs.

FEATHER CARE

Birds have different kinds of feathers. Contour feathers are what most people think of when feathers come to mind. These feathers have a hollow central shaft with vanes on either side. The vanes are made up of individual filaments that hook together with tiny barbs. Contour feathers give birds their shape, color, and markings; specialized contour feathers on the wings allow the birds to fly. Down feathers are shorter than contour feathers and have no barbs to hold the filaments together. The down feathers are found underneath the contour feathers. The fluffy down feathers trap air near the bird's skin, where it is warmed by body heat. Some birds, such as pigeons, herons, and hawks, have specialized down feathers that disintegrate into powder as they grow.

Birds use their bills to preen, that is, to clean, rearrange, and oil their feathers. Preening also smoothes the feathers and closes any gaps. You will often see a bird "nibble" at its feathers to fasten the tiny barbs of the vane filaments together. Birds use their bills to take oil from the preen gland located on their rumps and spread it over their feathers to keep them waterproof and flexible. Birds that produce powder down distribute it over their feathers to aid in waterproofing.

Passerine birds often take baths by splashing in shallow water. The primary purpose of bathing is to rid the feathers of old preen oil and dirt. To rid themselves of ectoparasites such as mites, ticks, fleas, and lice, small birds such as wrens and sparrows also take dust baths. These birds find areas of loose, dry soil and "bathe" in them, behaving as if the soil were water.

Anting is an intriguing passerine bird behavior. You may sometimes see a bird pick up an ant and rub it over its body; birds also sometimes squat down over anthills and let the ants swarm over their bodies. Exactly why the birds do this is not fully understood. Current thinking is that the ants secrete substances that kill fungus on feathers and may also kill parasites.

As feathers wear out, they loosen in their sockets; new feathers growing in from within the socket push the old feathers out, a process called "molting." Most birds molt once or twice a year over a period of one to two months before and after the breeding season. This is how they acquire—and lose—their breeding plumage. Hawks molt much more slowly, taking as long as two years to replace all their feathers. This process often allows birders to identify individual resident birds by their conspicuously missing tail or primary feathers.

Ducks, grebes, swans, and some other birds molt all at once (synchronous molting), to the point that they can't fly for a few weeks.

Display Behavior

Display behavior consists of predictable actions by birds in response to specific situations. Display behavior can be divided roughly into two categories: territorial and courtship. In these circumstances, a bird will display its plumage or some other conspicuous characteristic and engage in a series of stylized actions, often accompanied by specific vocalizations. (Bird sounds are discussed in chapter 4 as well.)

Observing display behavior is a very good way to identify birds, both by the behavior itself and by the good look at field marks the behavior offers. Head crests, for instance, are usually very visible during territorial encounters.

Territorial displays

A territorial display is a predictable action by a bird used to define its territory or to defend it in response to an incursion. Among the passerines, a bird's territory is generally all or part of its home range: the area in which it courts, breeds, feeds, and carries on all its other usual activities. Among gulls and other birds that nest in dense colonies, territory is sometimes as small as the area just around the nest. No matter what the territory's size, birds actively defend it against intruders of the same species. (Remember that different species can occupy the same habitat if they use different niches.) Thus, a lot of territorial behavior is virtually indistinguishable from aggressive behavior. At the same time, because establishing and defending a territory are crucial to attracting a mate, the displays and actions used in territorial displays are often very similar or even identical to those used in courtship displays and in defending the nest. Often you must be aware of the context of the behavior in order to assess it correctly. Territorial behavior generally is strongest in the spring and early summer as the birds compete for mates and then raise their young. It tends to become less intense after this time.

Many birds, especially the passerines, use song or other sound (woodpecker drumming, for instance) to define the boundaries of their territories. Like song, finding and defending a territory are a male function almost exclusively.

Aggressive territorial behavior is often signaled by the bird's posture. An annoyed Canada Goose, for example, stretches its neck out horizontally, holds its head down low, and hisses. Many passerines also use a horizontal posture, with the head forward and the wings slightly spread, during aggressive encounters.

Another form of territorial behavior is the display of conspicuous plumage or other features. Red-winged Blackbirds, for example, perch to sing in a conspicuous spot such as the top of a cattail and flash their vivid red shoulder patches. In aggressive encounters, meadowlarks flash the white outer feathers of their wings and tail; Eastern Kingbirds fan their tails to display the white margin. Tufted Titmice, when threatened, raise their head crests. Many birds puff out their feathers, raise their crests, fan their tails, spread their wings, and otherwise take actions that make their bodies look larger and more threatening. When they do, you can usually get a good look at the markings and colors of the plumage.

Flight displays are sometimes used to indicate territory. Red-winged Blackbirds will glide slowly from one perch to another around the boundaries of their territory, flashing their shoulder epaulets the entire time. Other birds such as Northern Mockingbirds sometimes fly out from a perch on the border of the territory, make a short loop, and come back to the perch. Hummingbirds can be surprisingly aggressive in defense of their territory, swooping repeatedly in loops to drive off other birds and predators. Killdeer make circling flights over their territory while giving the characteristic *kill deer* call. Shorebirds use flight displays quite often because they can be seen easily in the open terrain. When observing a flight display, look for the same traits as when observing flight in general. In addition, look for the height and direction of the flight, listen for any calls during the flight, and watch for plumage displays. Don't stop watching after the bird lands. The display often continues with strutting, wing motions, and other behavior.

Other interesting, easily observed forms of territorial behavior include bill-waving or tilting, head-bobbing, and bowing. You can readily see this sort of behavior and most other forms of territorial and aggressive behavior by observing the birds at your feeder or the pigeons in a park. You can also easily see appeasement behavior here as birds respond to threatening behavior by retreating, often with their heads lowered and turned away.

If an intruding bird doesn't get the message from the display behavior, the defending bird may escalate its defenses to

Male Red-winged Blackbirds in the breeding season are very territorial. As they patrol their territory or sing to define and defend it, they flash their bright-red shoulder patches.

The male Great Egret grows magnificent head, neck, and scapular plumes during the breeding season. This bird was hunted nearly to extinction in the late 1800s for its plumes. In the 1890s women members of the growing new Audubon movement saved the Great Egret by making feathers unfashionable. In 1909 President Theodore Roosevelt protected the bird's habitat by designating Pelican Island in Florida as the first national wildlife refuge.

the point of chasing or actually attacking the intruder. These encounters are fairly common. Feathers may fly, and there may be a lot of noise, but serious harm is rare. Sometimes backyard birds will mistake their own reflection in a window for the presence of an invader. Because the "invader" doesn't respond to the usual territorial displays, the bird ends up attacking the reflection.

COURTSHIP DISPLAYS

After a female bird is attracted to the male's territory, he begins to court her with special display behavior. Courtship displays can take many forms, some quite spectacular or elaborate.

One form of courtship display is breeding (sometimes called "nuptial") plumage. This is the colorful, sometimes quite elaborate plumage that a male bird develops during the breeding season. The special plumes that a male Great Egret grows to attract a female are so spectacular that the bird was hunted nearly to extinction for them in the late 1800s.

Flight, often accompanied by sounds or vocalizations, is an important component of courtship displays for many birds. Many raptors perform spectacular acrobatics in the air. Birds such as meadowlarks, found in open areas that lack high perches, hover in the air and sing their songs. Hummingbirds swoop back and forth in large arcs while making chirping noises. These birds position themselves so that the sunlight strikes their iridescent plumage and shows the colors off to best advantage. Woodcocks gather at dusk in open areas called "leks." The females watch as the males soar high into the air and then plummet downward, giving a characteristic *peent* call

Great Blue Herons have elaborate courtship displays involving dancing, skypointing (as the bird on the right is doing), and short flights, accompanied by bill snapping. The largest heron in North America, the Great Blue usually breeds in colonies of dozens or more birds.

as they fall. An interesting aspect of lekking behavior is that it takes place year after year in the same place, making it easy for birders to schedule a visit. Lekking behavior can be seen in other species as well, including grouse, which exhibit ritualized dancing behavior. Prairie Chickens, Sharp-tailed Grouse, and Sage Grouse perform strutting and stamping motions on leks while making booming or popping noises with the air sacs on their necks or chests.

Dancing is part of the courtship ritual for many shorebirds, cranes, and herons. Dancing can involve a number of stylized behaviors, including jumping, executing wing movements, pointing the bill, "curtseying," and presenting food or nesting materials.

Waterbirds such as ducks often chase each other as part of their courtship behavior. Ducks also do a sort of dance, splashing in the water and performing exaggerated head and neck motions. Grebes have amazing courtship displays that involve, among other behaviors, synchronized displays of mating birds rushing together across the surface of the water.

An excellent way to see stylized courtship behavior is to watch colonial birds such as Great Blue Herons. These large, angular birds build bulky platform nests of sticks in trees in wetland areas; they are quite tolerant of human observation. As part of its courtship behavior, the male bird brings sticks to the nest and presents them to the female with stylized motions that include bowing, stamping, and croaking or hissing vocalizations. He may also make short, circular flights from the nest. Many scientists believe that modern birds are direct descendants of the dinosaurs. When watching and hearing the activity at a heronry at dusk, it is almost possible to imagine yourself back in the Jurassic period.

Among most passerines, courtship behavior is generally less extravagant. Males usually display to the females with characteristic behavior, which could include chasing, bowing, strutting, spreading the wings and tail, and presenting nesting materials. A few common birds, such as Northern Cardinals, perform courtship feeding. The female cardinal stands next to the male and begs for food by shivering her wings and making a special call. The male responds by gently placing a seed in her bill. One of the best ways to observe typical courtship behavior is to watch park pigeons. These birds display quite obviously throughout the year.

NESTING AND PARENTAL BEHAVIOR

As with other aspects of bird life, nesting and parental behavior vary greatly from species to species, ranging from practically nonexistent to very involved.

Birders need to be particularly careful when watching nesting and parental behavior. Birds that are disturbed or harassed before they have laid their eggs may desert the nesting site. If this happens, the birds may then have to nest in a less desirable place or skip breeding altogether. Never watch a nest site for more than a few minutes. If your presence is disturbing the birds, leave immediately. In heavily birded areas, it might be a good idea not to watch nest sites at all. Your few minutes, combined with the few minutes of every other birder in the area, might be too much for the birds. Be extremely careful not to disturb any vegetation around a nest. By breaking a branch off to get a better view for yourself, you might also reveal the nest to a predator such as a raccoon or snake.

If you see birds carrying nesting materials (feathers, twigs, mud, grass, or plant fibers) or insects to feed the young, try following them to find the nest. You may not have much luck. Many, though not all, nesting birds are very stealthy, often quietly taking circuitous routes to well-concealed nests. Blue Jays, ordinarily raucous and very visible, practically disappear during their nesting season. Many birds exhibit caution displays as they approach their nests, especially if they know that predators or humans are watching. Look for birds that are behaving nervously by sitting very erect, flicking their wings and tails, wiping their bills, and performing other fidgety actions. This behavior tells you that the bird knows you are there. If you feel you are preventing the bird from tending to its nest, leave.

Taking the habitat approach to nesting sites is often more productive. Look in places where the bird is likely to nest and listen for the sounds of contact calls from the adults and peeps from the chicks. Phoebes commonly nest on sheltered ledges and house porches; House Finches are fond of ornamental evergreens. Look for small, round holes in the trunks of large, dead trees to find cavity nesters such as woodpeckers and chickadees. Also listen for the sound of woodpecker drumming because these birds often do this near the nest site. Don't try to peer through the leaves and branches of bushes and dense vegetation. Crouch down, put your head under the bush at ground level, and look up. Despite all your maneuvering, you may not see the nest. As the leaves fall in the autumn, you will see a surprising number of nests that you never noticed in the spring and summer, even at places you visited often.

DISTRACTION DISPLAYS

While walking through a field with your dog in the late spring, you come across an injured Killdeer that flutters along, dragging one wing pathetically and giving pitiful chirps. Your dog gives chase, and you follow to prevent mayhem, only to see the bird suddenly fly off normally. The Killdeer has just successfully lured you away from its nest with a distraction display. Feigning injury is a common distraction display among ground-nesting birds such as Spotted Sandpipers, Killdeer, and many shorebirds and waterfowl.

Another form of distraction display is "rodent running." Here the bird distracts a potential predator such as a coyote from the nest by running off in a rodent-like manner. Rodent running is seen mostly in rails and shorebirds.

Migration Behavior

For centuries, bird migration was deeply mysterious. Where did the birds go when they disappeared for months on end? Until well into the nineteenth century, some observers believed that swallows hibernated at the bottom of ponds, like frogs. Today we know a lot more about bird migration, but many unanswered questions remain. Whatever the reasons for it, bird migration provides fabulous birdwatching.

Migration periods

Most migratory birds head south in September and October and north in April and May. These are very approximate times, however, because some of the birds that breed in the Arctic have started south again by the end of July. When birds return north from their wintering areas in Central and South America and points even farther afield, they arrive in North America starting in March. Obviously these birds will arrive in Canada several weeks later.

Many passerines migrate at night, when the air is smoother and predators are few, landing at daybreak to feed and rest.

Raptors migrate by day to take advantage of thermals and resting passerines.

Flyways

Migrating birds follow four main paths, or flyways, in both directions: the Atlantic coast, the Pacific coast, the Mississippi River, and the central states. At points along these routes, natural features such as mountains can concentrate the birds, but generally the migration routes are across broad fronts that are very wide. Migration patterns along the Pacific coast are somewhat less well defined, but by positioning yourself in any flyway during migration, you will see a lot of birds. Most birding hot spots are located along flyways.

Migrant traps

Migrant traps are areas of suitable bird habitat surrounded by areas of unsuitable habitat—a waterhole in a desert, for example. A well-known migrant trap is Central Park in New York City. In the spring, hungry, tired birds spot this oasis of green in a desert of concrete and come in for a landing. Well over two hundred species have been seen in the park. Migrant traps are found everywhere, although you may need local knowledge to find them—another good reason to join your local bird club. Birding hotlines (see chapter 7) are a great way to find out about migrant traps and what birds are in them at any given time.

6

SEEING MORE BIRDS

After you've mastered the basic principles of bird identification and have a good start on your life list, you're ready to see more birds by identifying some of the trickier species and venturing farther afield.

WARBLERS

Watching warblers is a great aesthetic pleasure and a great identification headache. For beginners, part of the problem is simply that there are so many warbler species. As with other aspects of birding, approach the situation systematically, and the confusion will lessen somewhat.

Warblers (or wood warblers, to distinguish them from Old World warblers, family Sylviidae) are found only in the New World. There are fifty-four members of the Parulidae and Peucedramidae families, divided into seventeen genera, found north of the Rio Grande. Some, such as the Yellow Warbler, are widespread; others, such as Townsend's Warbler, have somewhat restricted ranges; a few, such as the Colima Warbler, have very restricted ranges. All warblers are migratory; many spend the winter in the tropics.

Warbler identification is easiest in the spring, when the males are in their colorful and distinctive breeding plumage and sing often. Warblers in the spring tend to travel in small, mixed flocks.

Warblers are often first spotted by their size and behavior. These small, active birds are most often seen darting around looking for insects in overgrown areas having low trees, brushy undergrowth, and water. Your first impression of a warbler will usually be of a small, flitting bird with some yellow on it—most but by no means all warblers are fairly colorful. After you've spotted a warbler, try to get a good look at its head, throat, and breast. Don't bother looking at the bill because you already know that the bird has a long, thin one. Instead, note the colors and markings. The stunning Blackburnian Warbler, for instance, has a striking orange throat and head when in full breeding plumage. Next, try to spot the wings. The Blue-winged Warbler is mostly yellow, with dusky blue-gray wings. Next, look for colors on the throat and rump. An excellent example here is the aptly named Yellow-rumped Warbler, which is grayish all over but has both a bright yellow throat and a bright yellow rump patch, along with prominent white wing bars. This is one of the most common and easy-to-spot warblers—get to know it as a reference bird.

Note where the bird is within the habitat. Warblers search for food at various levels within the woods, a phenomenon known as "layering," or stratigraphic preference. In a classic ornithological study, the distinguished ecologist Robert MacArthur discovered that five different warblers apparently sharing the same niche actually occupied different layers of the habitat. MacArthur studied the foraging habits in conifers of the Cape May, Yellow-rumped, Black-throated Green, Bay-breasted, and Blackburnian Warblers. Each warbler foraged for insects in a separate part of the tree; in addition, each warbler foraged in a somewhat different manner.

In practical terms, layering means that if you see where in the habitat the bird is, you have an important clue to its identity. High-level warblers are found toward the tops of the tallest trees; mid-level warblers are found in the bottom two-thirds of tall trees and the tops of small trees and undergrowth. Low-level warblers are found below eye level down to the ground. Your field guide will often, but not always, mention a warbler's stratigraphic preference. The guide will also probably mention the bird's habitat preference. Cape May Warblers prefer conifers and flowering trees; Prairie Warblers prefer low, brushy areas and second-growth woods. Like all birds, warblers will sometimes be found outside their preferred habitat, but, on the whole, they know what they like and will be found there most often. This is a big help in identification because it lets you quickly eliminate species that aren't usually found in a particular habitat.

When you watch warblers, the action is often very fast. Don't take the time to look up each bird in your field guide as you see it—you could easily miss other birds in the meantime. As it is, in the time it takes you to get your binocs on the bird, it may well flit away.

Listen carefully for songs. Warblers, despite their name, don't really warble; their songs are often complex but aren't particularly musical. Each species does have a distinctive, usually high-pitched, and often buzzy or trilled song. If you can identify the song, you have identified the bird. Some of the most common warbler songs, such as those of the Ovenbird and Prairie Warbler, are easy to learn; others are more challenging. Listen to the recordings, watch the videos, and try to hear the birds singing in the field.

Warblers in autumn are even more of a challenge. By the time warblers are ready to head south again, their colorful breeding plumage and distinctive patterns have faded, although their most prominent field marks are still dimly visible and may be enough to give you a good identification clue.

Immature birds have not yet reached adult plumage and are also drably colored; female birds never have the same bright colors and markings as males. Every field guide shows breeding, nonbreeding, and female plumage, but the pictures aren't always much help. If you can't identify a confusing fall warbler, don't worry about it—you are very far from alone.

SHOREBIRDS

Shorebirds are hard for everyone, not just beginners, to identify. You may not believe this as your field trip leader quickly and confidently identifies four different sandpipers standing on a mud flat while you are still trying to get a handle on just one, but even the leader was a beginner once.

To watch shorebirds, use a spotting scope if possible. Shorebirds are skittish, and you often can't get close enough for your binoculars to give you the detail you need to see the birds well and attempt an identification. But on the other hand, behavior is an important clue, and you should be able to observe this easily with binoculars.

Focus on standing birds. Most shorebirds in flight are hard to identify, with some exceptions, such as the striking white

During high tide, shorebirds such as these Semipalmated Sandpipers tend to huddle together and rest. For birders, this is a chance to get a good look at the birds while they're holding still.

wing pattern seen when a Willet takes flight. Why try, when most of the birds are standing within easy scoping range? Home in on a small group of birds and look carefully at each one. Chances are they are mostly all the same species, with a few individuals of different species mixed in with the crowd. Work on identifying the most numerous species; you can then work out the oddballs by process of elimination. Be patient and systematic. The shorebirds aren't going anywhere in particular, so take your time.

To begin placing a shorebird into its proper family, look first at its overall shape. Note its silhouette, bill shape, and bill length. Look especially for birds with very long legs, very long bills, or a plump, roundish shape. Before you head to the coast or the wetlands, study the shorebird silhouettes found in your field guide. With a little homework and some practice, you will soon be able to distinguish the families. This doesn't necessarily get you too far because most of the birds you see will be one of the eight common plovers (family Charadriidae) or one of the thirty-eight common sandpipers (family Scolopacidae). The sandpiper family includes the easily recognized curlews and godwits, but also includes the "peeps," six very similar small sandpiper species. Of the other common shorebirds, the two oystercatchers (family Haematopodidae) are easily recognized, as are the American Avocet and Black-necked Stilt (family Recurvirostridae).

Next, consider the habitat. Shorebirds have distinct preferences: Some are found on sandy beaches, others on coastal mud flats, and others in freshwater marshes. Your field guide will mention the species' preferred habitat.

After you have sorted the birds into basic categories, you can try to go further. Here's where it gets really hard. The biggest problem is plumage because a shorebird could be wearing one of several variations, depending on its age, sex, and breeding status. Males and females of most shorebirds look much alike. Your field guide depicts adult birds in full summer breeding plumage (also called "basic plumage") and full winter plumage (also called "alternate" or, rarely, "eclipse plumage"). Unfortunately, the birds are often in transitional stages between seasonal plumages. In addition, young shorebirds could be in juvenile plumage (first plumage after the downy

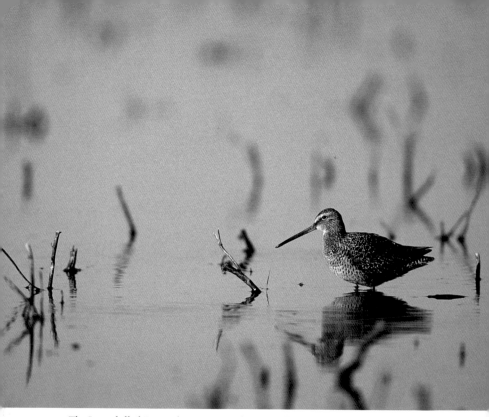

The Long-billed Dowitcher is a typical cryptically colored shorebird, especially in nonbreeding plumage (in breeding plumage, this bird has a rufous belly, making it a little easier to identify). Keep watching and listening; a good way to identify this bird is by its sharp keek flight call and by the constant soft chattering noise a feeding flock makes.

stage), first winter plumage (not the same as adult winter plumage), or first summer plumage (not the same as adult breeding plumage). To make it all even more confusing, shorebirds all tend toward the same tans, grays, browns, and buffs in cryptic patterns. When watching shorebirds, try to identify them by shape and behavior, not plumage. Ditto for leg color—the legs are often hard to see, immersed in water, or caked with sand or mud. If you are interested in shorebirds, lots of good identification hints are found in the pages of advanced guides and specialized books. A good introduction is *The Shorebird Guide* by Michael O'Brien, Richard Crossley, and Kevin Karlson.

Gulls and Terns

The good news here is that it is relatively easy to distinguish between gulls and terns (all members of the Laridae family), based on all the usual field marks: shape, tail (terns have forked tails), bill, color, and feeding behavior.

Beyond that, identification gets a little trickier. The terns are complicated, but the field marks and distribution patterns are fairly clear. Study your field guide to learn the marks and then practice.

Gulls such as this Laughing Gull can have six different plumages, depending on age. The bird here has only a faint gray streak of black on its head and a black bill, indicating a nonbreeding adult. COURTESY OF SUSAN DAY/DAYBREAK IMAGERY

The Laughing Gull shown here is an adult in full breeding plumage, including the black hood, reddish bill, and thin, white partial eye ring. COURTESY OF ROBERT MCKEMIE/DAYBREAK IMAGERY

For gulls, you will need to apply all your basic birding ID skills along with the ability to remember as many as five to nine different plumages for each species. Gull identification is too complex to deal with here, particularly because it is the author's biggest weakness as a birder (after shorebirds—inland birders don't have many opportunities to practice). Advanced guides, such as *Peterson Reference Guide to Gulls of the Americas* by Steve Howell and Jon Dunn, discuss and illustrate the topic exhaustively.

Beginning birders should particularly note that there is no such bird as a seagull.

Pelagic Birding

If you want to fill in all those blanks at the start of your check-list, you will have to go on a pelagic birding trip. "Pelagic" means "ocean-going"; to see these birds, you must be ocean-going yourself, preferably on a chartered boat with a lot of like-minded birders. Many birding clubs and organizations arrange pelagic trips. They can be a little expensive, especially if you live inland and must travel to meet the boat very early in the morning, but they are definitely worth it. In addition to seeing shearwaters, petrels, gulls, terns, phalaropes, skuas, and other great birds, you may also see whales.

Dress warmly for a pelagic trip and bring a waterproof outer layer—the wind and weather 50 miles offshore can be very cold and wet even in the summer. A pelagic trip tends to be an all-day event, so bring ample food and drink. Bring your most powerful binoculars but leave your spotting scope at home. Even with a shoulder mount, the deck will move too much for a scope to be useful.

That moving deck will also probably make you seasick at some point during the trip. You will have plenty of company as you hang over the stern rail. The chances of seasickness are reduced if you stay on deck, keep your eyes on the horizon, and keep busy. This is easy to do on a pelagic trip because the whole point is to scan the horizon looking for birds. And nothing will make you forget how lousy you feel faster than catching sight of a new bird.

Counterintuitive as it may sound, it also helps to keep your stomach full. Eat plain, easily digested foods such as apples, crackers, rolls, and the like. Avoid anything very sweet, greasy, or fried. Even if you have to force yourself, drink plenty of water or fruit juice; avoid alcohol and carbonated drinks. Also avoid looking at or getting downwind of the chum (a loathsome mixture of ripe fish heads and guts) that is sometimes dumped overboard to draw birds closer.

Nonprescription medications for motion sickness can make you drowsy, which will not do much for your birding. Some people swear by acupressure bracelets or ginger. If you know you have a real problem with seasickness, ask your doctor about prescription medications.

NESTING COLONIES

Many pelagic birds, particularly gulls, terns, and alcids (auks), breed in crowded colonies on rocky islands and sheer cliffs near the ocean. Thousands upon thousands of birds—some colonies may have a quarter of a million members—nest right next to each other. The sheer numbers, the distinctive aroma, and the incredible cacophony add up to a memorable experience.

On the East Coast, colonies of puffins, murres, guillemots, gannets, gulls, kittiwakes, and other birds are found on the rocky coasts of the maritime provinces (New Brunswick, Nova Scotia, and Prince Edward Island), Newfoundland, the Gaspé Peninsula of Quebec, and in northern Maine. On the West Coast, look for nesting colonies along the rocky Pacific Northwest coastline and Alaska. In addition to gulls, puffins, murres, guillemots, and other birds, auklets and murrelets can also be seen. As a bonus, you may also see Bald Eagles, ospreys, seals, whales, and other wildlife.

Many nesting colonies can be seen from land or from the many ferries that travel in these regions (particularly among the maritime provinces and along the magnificent coast of British Columbia). Unless you have or are with someone with local knowledge of the waters, it's not a good idea to visit a nesting island on your own; in fact, it may not be legally possible. Many birding organizations and tour operators arrange boat trips to nesting colonies; check organization and tourism Web sites and look in the pages of the birding magazines for announcements. Be absolutely certain to wear a broad-brimmed hat if you visit a nesting colony.

Owling

Virtually all your birdwatching takes place during the day. Owling is the art of seeking out owls when they are most active—at night. An owling trip actually starts days before with scouting trips to locate owl roosts. Pick a likely patch of habitat (check your field guide) and explore it for signs of owls. Listen for hoots. Look for roosting places by watching for splashes of "whitewash" (owl excrement) or pellets (regurgitated indigestible matter) under tree branches. Check into rock crevices, tree cavities, and other possible roosting places. Owls tend to prefer dense vegetation and are often found in thick conifer woods.

To catch the owl in action, trade your binoculars for a powerful flashlight with fresh batteries. Dress warmly. For optimal results, time your excursion for well after midnight, preferably the couple of hours before dawn. If you want to go owling at a more manageable hour, begin just at dusk. Early

Owls are masters of camouflage. This Screech Owl is so well concealed that it could easily be overlooked by a birder scoping out birds for an owling expedition. Look for other owl signs, such as whitewash, to reveal a possible roosting place.

spring is a particularly good time because the birds are staking out territories and nesting sites and will be more active. Irruptive owls, of course, will be seen only in the winter. Whenever you look for owls, try to select a clear, calm, moonlit night. (If you go owling at dusk in the summer, you are also likely to see members of the nocturnal goatsucker family such as the Whippoor-will or Common Nighthawk.)

Walk quietly to the site you have staked out, using the flashlight to see the way. After you reach the site, turn off the light, get comfortable, and wait. You can try playing a recording of the owl's call to draw it in, but, if you are near a favorite roosting or calling site, it will turn up sooner or later on its own. Owls fly silently, so keep your eyes open for silhouettes swooping through the shadowy darkness.

To identify the owl (if you haven't already from hearing its vocalizations during your advance scouting), look for four basic clues: size, head shape, iris color, and plumage. Many owls are amazingly tame, sitting quietly while you approach to within a few feet. You should be able to see the details quite clearly.

There are only nineteen owl species in North America, and you can eliminate most on the basis of range and habitat. Within your narrowed field, look for size first. Owls range from very large (Great Horned Owl) to very small (Northern Saw-whet Owl). Irruptions of Arctic owls (most often Snowy and Great Gray) are fairly common, with the birds seen regularly in northern tier states such as Minnesota and Michigan. Individuals occasionally wander even farther south.

Examining an owl pellet gives you a pretty precise idea of what the bird has been eating. To study a pellet, break it into pieces and let it soak in a bowl of water for an hour or two. Then, using tweezers, gently pull the pieces apart in the water. Owl pellets generally contain the fur and bones of small mammals, although the feathers, claws, and beaks of birds are also sometimes found. The various types of bones can be readily recognized. Long bones are from the legs; curved bones are ribs; flat, jagged fragments are parts of the skull or shoulder; bills, teeth, jawbones, and vertebrae are unmistakable.

HAWKWATCHING

Hawks are masters of the air, soaring and flying with incredible power and grace. They are also relatively easy to find, watch, and identify, which makes them particularly good for honing your birding skills.

The easiest way to see a lot of hawks is to look for them during the autumn migration. Starting in August and continuing through November, migrant raptors stream south down well-defined migration routes. Migrating raptors tend to follow either coastlines or mountain ridges. In the eastern United States, two of the very best hawkwatching lookouts are Cape May Point on New Jersey's Atlantic coast and Hawk Mountain Sanctuary on the Kittatinny Ridge in the Allegheny Mountains of Pennsylvania. On a typical windy autumn day at Hawk Mountain, over 24,000 raptors of sixteen species may pass by. An extra bonus is that other migrating birds also pass by.

At any point along the migration routes, you may spot a flock of hawks soaring upward together in a tight spiral. What you are seeing is called a "kettle" or "boil." The hawks are using an updraft of warm air—a thermal—to rise effortlessly into the air.

Raptor identification requires you to take a step beyond basic identification by field marks. Generally speaking, you'll never see the birds closely enough to spot the diagnostic field marks. Raptors in flight must be identified by their flight. This usually means looking at the shape and characteristic position of the wings and the way the birds fly—the rhythm of their wing flaps and glides—to arrive at a strong overall impression, reinforced by any behavior or field marks you might see.

The very common Red-tailed Hawk is the reference bird for raptors. It's an easy bird to learn. Look for the characteristic rusty red tail feathers and stocky body. In flight, Red-tailed Hawks have stiff wingbeats and soar with the wings held in a slight dihedral; when they are gliding, the wings are level with the body with no dihedral.

Because so many hawks go by during migration time, you will have ample opportunity to learn.

Accipiters such as Sharp-shinned Hawks have long tails and relatively short, stubby wings. Buteos, such as the very common Red-tailed Hawk, have shorter tails and wider wings designed for soaring. Falcons are designed for speed, with long, pointed wings and long tails. The Northern Harrier has slimmer wings and a longer tail than buteos and is larger than accipiters.

Prepare for an autumn visit to a hawkwatch by studying your field guide and the indispensable book *Hawks in Flight* by Pete Dunne, David Sibley, and Clay Sutton. Pay particular attention to the silhouette drawings of birds in flight. Study the appearance of the Red-tailed Hawk because this is a benchmark bird. Review the names of the wing parts and feathers—you'll be hearing a lot about wrist patches and primaries. Dress warmly. Bring your binoculars, a hat with a brim, sunglasses, lip balm, and a cushion to sit on. The hawks go past all day long; bring food and drink. If you can, pick a day with a brisk northwest wind.

You will rarely be alone at a hawkwatching site. This is great for beginners because there will always be someone who can identify the birds as they pass over and point out the differences and similarities to you. At many hawkwatch sites, staff members give short identification classes for beginners. Captive birds are often on hand to give close-up looks.

Hawkwatchers tend to use a shorthand vocabulary. A "TV" is a Turkey Vulture; a "BV" is a Black Vulture; an "RTH" is Red-tailed Hawk. "Sharpie" is short for "Sharp-shinned Hawk."

"Dihedral," a term borrowed from aviation, is used to describe the position of the wings of a flying raptor. It usually describes the position of the wings relative to the body when the bird is seen head on in a gliding position. Technically, the dihedral is the angle formed between the wing and true horizontal or, in practical terms, the wings and the body. The dihedral is a helpful tool for identification. TVs, for instance, usually have a V-shaped dihedral; RTHs have a much flatter dihedral, with the wings almost horizontal. Kiting—holding

The Turkey Vulture soars with its wings held in a very distinctive V-shaped dihedral.

still while facing into the wind, like a kite on the end of a string—is another identification tool; it's often done by kestrels and Red-tailed and Ferruginous Hawks. "Hawk food" refers to any small, unidentified bird.

DESERT BIRDING

Technically, a desert is an arid region with a limited population of specially adapted plant and animal life. By this definition, a tundra is a cold desert. In practice, "desert birding" refers loosely to birdwatching in hot, dry areas with low or scrubby vegetation. The chaparral areas of southern California, the hilly piñon and juniper regions of the Southwest, the sage-brush hills of Nevada and Wyoming, and the true scrub desert of the Southwest and Texas are all great places for seeing birds. And because southern California, Arizona, New Mexico, and the Rio Grande Valley of Texas border on Mexico, you have a good chance of seeing birds that usually breed in Mexico but are sometimes found in the United States. In mountainous southeastern Arizona, for example, you could see ten or more hummingbird species, as well as Elegant and Eared Trogons.

You can easily predict the presence of some birds in arid areas simply by their names: Cactus Wren, Sage Thrasher, Western Scrub Jay, Pinyon Jay. Other common desert birds are Greater Roadrunner, Canyon Wren, Elf Owl, Common Poorwill, and Vermilion Flycatcher. The Southwest and the Rio Grande Valley cover a vast area. To get the most out of a birding trip, invest in one of the excellent bird-finding guides to the region and check the state and local tourism Web sites.

To have a safe and productive trip, follow a few simple pre-cautions. Dress for the weather and the terrain. Wear sturdy, ankle-high hiking boots. Lightweight clothing is essential for hot days but remember that desert areas, particularly those at high elevations, cool off rapidly at night. Bring a sweater or jacket. Wear a hat with a brim, wear sunglasses, and use plenty of sunscreen and lip balm. Bring lots of water—much more than you think you'll need—and be sure to drink it. At high elevations, the temperature may not feel that hot, but the air is very dry, and you can become dehydrated without feeling overheated or thirsty.

Cartoon birds don't usually have much in common with their real-life originals. The Greater Roadrunner, a common bird of the Southwest desert, is indeed very fast, running in pursuit of prey at speeds up to 18 miles an hour. Its characteristic call, however, is a sort of dovelike cooing, not beep-beep.

If you're birding by yourself, be sure to have a reliable vehicle and an accurate map, particularly if you're going into a remote or rugged area. Cell phone service will be spotty or nonexistent in wilderness areas. Tell someone where you're going and what your approximate schedule will be, in case of mishap.

TROPICAL BIRDING

Only one area of the continental United States is truly tropical: southern Florida. This region, which includes Everglades National Park, Biscayne National Park, Ding Darling National Wildlife Refuge at Sanibel Island, and the Keys, is a birder's paradise. Birds of all sorts are abundant and usually easy to see in southern Florida—a visit here is a great way to jumpstart your life list. Look especially for regional specialties among the shorebirds and waders, including Brown Pelican, Limpkin, Reddish Egret, Roseate Spoonbill, Wood Stork, and Purple Gallinules. Southern Florida also has some particular specialties, such as the Smooth-billed Ani and Gray Kingbird; the White-crowned Pigeon is found only in the Keys. Raptor watchers can hope to see Swallow-tailed Kites; the endangered Snail Kite can be seen at Lake Okeechobee and the Loxahatchee National Wildlife Refuge.

At the very tip of the chain of little islands that makes up the Florida Keys are several tiny islands called the Dry Tortugas. These keys are a six-hour (or more) boat ride into the Gulf of Mexico from Key West. They have no water, no accommodations aside from a very basic campground, and no other services of any sort, but they do have birds you can see nowhere else in the United States. Boobies, noddies, and tropicbirds

EXOTIC BIRDS

Many exotic (nonnative) species have been introduced into the United States over the years. Some were deliberate—sixty European Starlings were brought from Europe to Central Park in 1880 as part of a misguided effort to introduce all the birds mentioned in Shakespeare. These birds quickly established breeding populations that eventually spread over the entire continent, reaching the West Coast by 1950. Other introductions have been far less deliberate and less successful. Most exotic birds in the United States today are the descendants of escaped or released birds, particularly parrots, doves, and waterfowl, and most are found in areas with mild climates, particularly Florida and southern California. The Monk Parakeet, however, has managed to breed successfully for decades in some locations even in northern states such as Connecticut, New York, and Illinois. (A Monk Parakeet colony is found on the campus of Brooklyn College.)

After an exotic species becomes established, meaning it is self-sustaining (not dependent on human intervention) and breeds successfully, it will eventually be recognized by the American Birding Association and American Ornithologists' Union as part of the official birdlife of the region. That means it can be counted on your life list. In Florida you can count birds such as Eurasian Collared Dove, White-winged Parakeet, Common Myna, and Spot-breasted Oriole to your list. Other exotics, including many escaped parrot species, can be seen, particularly in the Miami region, but can't yet be counted.

are easily seen, and there is also a large colony of Sooty Terns. Because of the lack of facilities, it's best to visit the Dry Tortugas as part of a group. Trips are arranged by many birding organizations and tour operators; check online and in the pages of the birding magazines.

Numerous excellent bird-finding guides are available for Florida; online information abounds. Wherever you go to bird in Florida, bring sunscreen and plenty of insect repellent; you'll need them.

BACKYARD BIRDING

It's not really going afield to watch the birds in your own backyard, but it may be the easiest and most educational birding of all. Don't be put off by those who speak of backyard birders with derision. Some of the most original and important work on territoriality was done by Margaret Morse Nice, who observed the Song Sparrows in her Ohio backyard in the 1930s.

To observe the birds in your backyard, all you need do is look out your window. If you can put up a birdfeeder or a birdbath, so much the better. Even in large cities, you will attract a surprising variety of birds to go along with the starlings, House Sparrows, and pigeons. You can practice applying the principles of bird identification to the new birds you attract, but the real joy of backyard birding is observing bird behavior. Your house or apartment is the perfect observation blind—sheltered and temperate, with bathroom and kitchen at hand. By watching the yard regularly, you will soon start to observe territorial behavior, feeding patterns, aggression, mating behavior, and much more. You may also be fortunate enough to have robins, House Finches, Northern Cardinals, or other birds nest where they can easily be watched. You might even learn to recognize individual birds.

Another advantage of backyard birding is that you can get very close to the birds without disturbing their normal activity. If you put up a window feeder, for example, you will be able to watch the birds from only inches away. The intimate glimpses of bird life you see in your own backyard give you a deep qualitative understanding of a relatively few bird species. As you attain a more quantitative knowledge of birds, you will quickly recognize similar behavior in unfamiliar birds.

7

CHECKLISTS AND LISTS

Checklists, also known as "field cards" or "trip lists," are an easy way to keep track of what you see on a birding field trip. In its most basic form, a checklist is simply a listing, in taxonomic order, of every bird found at a particular site, with a space or box next to each listing. You check off (or tick, if you are British) each bird when and if you see it on your trip. Checklists are usually more complex than just a simple listing, but this is one of the rare instances where complexity is better than simplicity.

USING CHECKLISTS

At the main entrance to virtually any wildlife site—national and state parks, refuges, and sanctuaries—you will find a bird checklist in pamphlet form. Most are free; if there is a fee, it is nominal. You can usually also download the checklist in advance from the Web site. Having the checklist in advance makes it easier to plan your trip and know what to expect.

A thorough checklist for a birding site is crammed with useful information. It may contain a map of the site indicating lookout points, observation towers, trails, and bathrooms. Some background information about the site is also usually included. The checklist itself lists, in taxonomic order, only those birds that have been seen at the site. Next to each bird is an indication of its seasonal appearance, its status (e.g., migrant), and its relative abundance. A list of accidental and hypothetical (unconfirmed sightings) birds may also be included.

Seasonal appearance is usually divided into the four bird-watching seasons, as follows: Spring (abbreviated as "Sp" or "s") is March through May; summer (abbreviated "Su" or "S") is June through August; fall (abbreviated "F") is September through November; and winter (abbreviated "W") is December through February. Some checklists, particularly those along coastal flyways that get a lot of migrants, shorten summer to end in mid-July and divide autumn into two parts: Early fall (abbreviated "EF") is from mid-July to mid-September; late fall (abbreviated "LF") is from mid-September through November.

Status indicates the nature of a bird's presence at the site. Status categories are usually broken down as follows: "Permanent resident" (abbreviated "P") means that individuals of the species are present in all seasons; "migrant" (abbreviated "M") indicates species that move through the site in spring and autumn; "breeding" (abbreviated "B" or indicated by an asterisk or other symbol) means that the species is known to breed at the site; "transient" (abbreviated "T") indicates a nonbreeding species at the site as a temporary visitor (usually in the winter or summer).

Many checklists are fairly minimal and include only species, season, and status information. Some go beyond the basics and include a lot of other helpful information.

Relative abundance is an indication of the number of individuals of a species likely to be seen. Abundance categories tend to be a little loose, but the following terms generally apply: "abundant," meaning that numbers of the bird are easily observed at any time; "common," meaning that the bird is very likely to be seen or heard during the proper season in suitable habitat; "uncommon," meaning that the bird is present during the proper season but may not be seen; "occasional," meaning that the bird is seen only a few times during a season; "scarce," meaning that the bird is seen only once every few seasons; "rare," meaning that the bird is usually not present and is seen at intervals of two to five years; and "accidental," meaning that there is only one existing record of the bird at the site.

The birds in the checklist are listed down the left-hand side of the page, with a space for the checkmark to the left of each species. The seasons are listed across the top of each page to the right of the species list. Status and abundance are indicated to the right of each species, under the appropriate season. Generally, the abbreviations discussed earlier are used, either singly or in combination, to indicate the relative abundance of a species during each season and its status. Sometimes the relative abundance is given in a more directly visual way by a horizontal bar across the seasons. The width of the bar from top to bottom indicates abundance. The thicker the bar, the more abundant the bird.

This may all sound more confusing than helpful but, to a beginning birder, a good checklist is a godsend. Glance over the checklist before beginning your field trip to get an idea of what to expect from the site. If you know from the checklist that you should be looking for breeding Glossy Ibis in the spring, for example, you are more likely to see them and to identify them immediately as Glossy Ibis. More importantly for beginners, the checklist helps you quickly eliminate your wilder guesses about a bird's identity. If you think you have spotted a Wilson's Phalarope at Jamaica Bay in late autumn, a glance at the checklist tells you that this bird is rare for the time and place. You can thus eliminate this bird from consideration and concentrate on figuring out what sort of sandpiper the bird really is (Black-necked Stilt, probably).

As a beginning birder, you may not be able to pin down your identifications to a species within a family. You may be able to identify a bird as a member of the wren family, for example, but not beyond that. In such cases, you should still make a checklist notation. In the margin near the family in question (or elsewhere if there isn't room), write "wren sp." (short for "species"). If you see more than one unidentified species, use the plural abbreviation "spp."

Perhaps the most important abbreviation a novice birder needs for a checklist is the frequently used "LBB," which stands for "little brown bird." Variations include "LYB" for "little yellow bird" and "LBJ" for "little brown job." Another common abbreviation is "BVD" for "better view desired." My personal favorite is "SCB," for "small chirpy bird." Don't be embarrassed to enter these on your checklist—if more experienced birders do it, so can you.

In addition to the information provided on the checklist, you should add some of your own. Note the number of individuals seen in a species—for example, you saw six Northern Cardinals or a flock of Canada Geese estimated at two hundred. If you can, indicate sex and age by your checkmarks. Note the date and time of your trip, the weather conditions, the route you took, with whom you went, any interesting behavior you may have seen, and anything else that seems relevant. Count up the total number of species seen and heard. If you see a life bird on the trip, you will certainly want to note that.

Your checklists contain lots of valuable information—never discard them. Checklists from previous visits to a particular site are very useful when you are planning a return trip. Use the old checklist to draw up a list of the birds you missed the last time, for example, or to decide on a different route.

Lists

Listing is an integral part of birdwatching, one that provides a great deal of harmless fun and also helps make you a better birder.

Life lists

Virtually all birders keep a life list—that is, a list of all the bird species they have ever seen. A fairly serious birdwatcher can easily have a life list that tops 300 species, whereas a really serious birder will have seen at least 500. A number of the best birders in North America have seen 700 or more of the 957 birds on the American Birding Association checklist. Phoebe Snetsinger of the United States, who devoted most of her life to the pursuit of birds, holds the world record for species seen. She had seen 8,450 species and was in pursuit of bird 8,451 when she was killed in a van accident in Madagascar in 1999.

As a beginner, you will probably want to concentrate on building up your life list, adding as many species as possible. This is fairly easy to do at first, when every bird is new to you, but you will slow down a bit after you get to the first hundred or so. To add new birds more quickly, you will probably have to travel outside your local area. To get much over two hundred life birds, you will certainly have to travel, at least within your state and probably farther afield.

Your life list should be more than just checkmarks on a preprinted list. Many birders keep detailed records about their life birds, including the date, time, place, circumstances, and sighting notes.

Follow these rules when adding birds to your lift list: Count only birds that you have seen or heard since you started the list. Add a bird to the list only if you feel you have positively identified it and would be able to identify it again. You can count a bird that was first seen or heard by someone else and pointed and identified for you but only if you saw or heard enough of the bird to note at least one diagnostic field mark or characteristic sound. Only unrestrained, native, living birds should be counted—captive or dead birds of any sort are out, as are escaped exotic and pet birds. Finally, count the bird only if it was observed under ethical conditions (see the ABA Code of Birding Ethics in Appendix A). In all aspects of listing, let your conscience be your guide.

LISTING REGIONS

Most birders actually keep two basic life lists: an American Birding Association Area List and a World List. The ABA checklist area includes Canada and the forty-nine continental United States and their adjacent waters to a distance of 200 miles or half the distance to a nonincluded area,

ABA CHECKLIST CODES

The American Birding Association assigns a checklist code to each species found in the ABA checklist area; the code indicates the rarity of the species.

Code 1 and Code 2 indicate regularly occurring North American birds, including regular breeding species and visitors. Code 1 species are more widespread and are usually more numerous; Code 2 species may have a more restricted North American range or may be widespread but occur at lower densities or behave in a very secretive way, making them difficult to detect. Code 3 means a species is rare, occurring in very low numbers but turning up every year in the ABA checklist area. Visitors and rare breeding residents usually get this code. Code 4 means "casual," a species that is not recorded every year in the ABA checklist area but has been recorded at least three times in the past thirty years. Code 5 means "accidental," a species that has been recorded only five times or fewer in the ABA checklist area and has fewer than three records in the past thirty years. Code 6 means the species can't be found in the checklist area at all. The species is probably or actually extinct or extirpated from the area.

whichever is less. The southern offshore limit is the latitude of the Mexican border. The birds of the ABA Area are defined by the ABA Checklist Committee. The birds of the world are defined by the latest edition of *Birds of the World: A Checklist* by James F. Clements. The sixth edition of this work, usually referred to in birders' shorthand as just Clements, was published in 2007.

In addition to the ABA checklist area, there are nine ABA listing regions: the six continents and their offshore waters and the three major oceans. By this definition, North America includes all of Canada and the continental United States below the Arctic Circle, the Caribbean region, and Mexico and the rest of Central America. (The Arctic is part of the Atlantic region; Hawaii is part of the Pacific region.)

The ABA listing areas are often broken down by listers into smaller, more manageable geographic subdivisions such as the lower forty-eight or fifty states, New England, and the like.

An alternative to the ABA checklist area is the checklist of North American birds published by the American Ornithologists' Union. Geographically, this list covers the region from the Arctic through Panama, including the West Indies and Hawaii. The AOU checklist also assigns a reference number to every species. These numbers are widely used in the ornithological world for scientific work, but they can be more than a little confusing to beginners.

OTHER LISTS

Listing can go far, far beyond the life list—Roger Tory Peterson kept a list of all the birds he had ever seen or heard in movies. The more usual sorts of lists are generally restricted by time, place, or some combination of the two. Many birders keep a year list, tallying all the species seen in a calendar year; they also often keep state or locality lists and a property or neighborhood list. Time and place lists can be narrowed further. Time lists, for example, could include seasonal totals, monthly totals, totals on a particular day from year to year, even birds seen on your birthday. For an extra fillip, you can calculate averages—the average number of birds you have seen in a month, for example. The shorter the time period, the more often you can enjoy recalculating the average.

Place lists could include birds seen in a particular refuge, in the neighborhood, in the county, on the way to and from the weekend house, on vacations, and the like. Even more limited are lists that combine time and place: all the birds seen in a particular park at lunchtime, in the backyard by month, or at a particular hot spot in the first week of May, for example.

Other interesting lists to keep include captive birds seen (in homes as pets, in zoos and aviaries, at banding stations), breeding birds, birds in flight, birds seen on television, juvenile birds, dead birds (museum specimens don't count), appearance lists (first and last appearance in a season), birds photographed, a list of all your birding lists, and virtually any other combination or permutation you can imagine.

What's the point of all this? For the more obsessive birders, listing has an intrinsic pleasure that needs no further explanation. If your personality tends toward this direction, you will find listing in all its variations to be an extremely satisfying aspect of birding. Even if you tend more to the haphazard, listing adds spice to birding and helps keep your enthusiasm high. It's always interesting to compare lists, such as those from the same day and place but different years. As you approach a listing milestone—your two hundredth bird, for example—an ordinary field trip can turn into a suspense-filled odyssey. (Definitely celebrate the attainment of a milestone.) Somehow even the most routine bird takes on new interest if seeing it means a checkmark on a list of your own devising—seeing a House Sparrow in every front yard in your neighborhood, say.

A gap in your list can make you redouble your efforts to see a particular bird. If you have seen every member of the heron family found in the East except for the American Bittern, for example, the unchecked box on your life list will haunt you until it is filled. And when it is filled, the mingled sense of joy and regret you feel is an emotion unique to birding.

BIRDING HOTLINES

The first rare bird alert, the Voice of Audubon, was begun in 1954 by the Massachusetts Audubon Society. Today many National Audubon Society local chapters, local independent Audubon societies, and other birding organizations have birding hotlines—recorded messages announcing general birding conditions in the region and details on where to find any rare and unusual birds that have been reported. The messages are changed at least once a week and often more frequently. The information is often quite detailed; have pen and paper handy to note directions and phone numbers. The expense to you is only the cost of the phone call. Most rare bird alerts are also now online; the phone messages remain as a way for birders in the field or away from home to call in.

The North American Rare Bird Alert (NARBA) is a fee-based service sponsored by the Houston Audubon Society. It provides information about sightings of unusual birds throughout North America, not just in a particular state or region. The phone number to hear the recorded message is given only to subscribers. Funds from NARBA subscriptions go to support an extensive system of refuges on the upper Texas coast. For more information, call (800) 458-BIRD or go to narba.org.

Some birders take "chasing," as rushing to see a rare or unusual bird is called, very seriously. They will drop everything at a moment's notice and travel hundreds if not thousands of miles to see (or not to see, as the case often is) the bird. As a beginning birder, you might think that you would never succumb to the chasing urge. All chasers were beginners once.

A complete and continuously updated list of North American birding hotlines is available on the American Birding Association Web site at aba.org.

Listing tools

Most field guides contain a basic taxonomic checklist in the back, but this is hardly adequate for even the most rudimentary life list, much less any other sort of list. The ABA official checklist of all 947 countable birds can be downloaded from the ABA Web site. State, regional, county, and site checklists can be downloaded from a wide variety of Web sites. The New York State Ornithological Association (nybirds.org), for instance, offers the official checklist of New York birds and links to regional and local checklists from birding groups around the state. Links to checklists for every national wildlife refuge can be found at the Northern Prairie Wildlife Research Center at npwrc.usgs.gov.

Printed checklists are great for use in the field, but most serious birders maintain their permanent life list on their computer using listing programs. These programs, from leading companies such as Thayer Birding Software or AviSys, are extremely sophisticated tools that are also very easy to use. The software isn't just for maintaining your birding records. You can use it to generate useful reports, plan trips, and learn

LIFE LISTS AND SCIENTISTS

Your life list and all your other birding lists are very personal. At the same time, they contain a wealth of information about appearance dates, ranges, breeding, and other aspects of bird life that can be very valuable for expanding scientific knowledge. eBird, a real-time, online checklist program launched in 2002 by the Cornell Laboratory of Ornithology and the National Audubon Society, amasses bird observations from amateurs and professionals alike to create a vast biodiversity data resource. Your observations, along with those of tens of thousands of others, help researchers build a better foundation for understanding bird distribution across the Western Hemisphere. It's easy to report your sightings to eBird using a simple interface; you can also use the site to maintain and analyze your personal bird records. Participation is free; sign up at ebirds.org.

more about birds through the pictures, recordings, and other detailed information included in the package. If you are planning a trip to a particular locale, your birding software can produce a report listing the birds found in the region, which of those birds you have already seen, and which you haven't. The target list of unseen species will help you set your goals and plan the trip. You can even download sound and video clips of your target birds to your iPod.

An alternative to purchasing your own birding software is to use Web sites that let you keep your lists online. These sites, such as chatterbirds.com and BirdingCentral.com, maintain your lists in the computing cloud—handy for accessing them if you're away from your own computer.

8

OPTICS FOR BIRDERS

Until quite recently, a birdwatcher's most important piece of equipment was a shotgun. John James Audubon, for example, routinely shot his specimens, stuffed them, and then used wires to arrange the corpses into lifelike positions for painting them. Ornithologists both before and after Audubon followed the same procedure, amassing study collections of bird specimens that are still of great value to modern researchers. Indeed, birds are sometimes still shot (the euphemism is "collected") for quite valid research purposes today.

MODERN OPTICS

In Audubon's day and for decades thereafter, telescopes and field glasses were cumbersome, heavy, and image distorting. Since the early 1900s, however, great improvements in optical engineering have led to binoculars and spotting scopes that are light and easy to use and provide sharp, accurate detail.

BINOCULARS

A really good pair of binoculars is the single most important investment a birdwatcher can make. Really good binoculars are expensive, running easily to well over a thousand dollars or more. As a beginner, you may be reluctant to spend that kind of money for superior optics when you can buy reasonably good ones for much less. Or you may already have binoculars that were obtained for some other reason years ago. You have a good point—if your commitment to birdwatching is of only the most casual sort. If it is anything more than that, spend the money.

The point of outstanding binoculars is not that you will see more birds—although you may—but rather that you will see them more accurately. Inexpensive optics distort the image and the colors. Just as a mediocre pianist sounds much better and enjoys it more when playing a fine grand piano than a battered upright, beginning birders find and identify more birds with good binoculars than poor ones.

It's also more cost effective to buy good binoculars at the start because you will buy them in the end anyway. Skip the inevitable period of increasing dissatisfaction and frustration that comes with crummy binoculars and go right for the good ones. Carefully chosen, high-quality binoculars can last a lifetime. As with any expensive purchase, be informed and shop around before you buy your new binocs. To help, following are short explanations of the important basic concepts and technical terms.

MAGNIFICATION

Binoculars are often described by their magnification and lens diameter, for example, "7 x 50." The first number in this description indicates the magnification. Thus, binoculars that magnify seven times (7x) will make objects appear to be seven times closer—that is, a bird that is 70 feet away will appear to be only 10 feet away when seen through the binoculars. Binoculars ranging from 7x to 10x are ideal for birding.

LENS DIAMETER

The second number in the description "7 x 50" indicates the diameter of the lens (also called the "objective") in millimeters (multiply by 0.04 for the equivalent in inches). Because bigger objectives gather more light, the larger the lens, the brighter the image and the better you can see in dim light. Bigger objectives also mean more resolution—you can see finer details. On the other hand, the bigger the objectives, the heavier the binoculars. Birders tend to choose binoculars that are in the range of 7 x 25, 7 x 50, 8 x 42, or 10 x 42. These sizes offer good compromises among magnification, brightness, and weight. Anything larger than 10 x 42 will be too heavy to use in the field.

FIELD OF VIEW

The size, expressed in degrees (angular field) or feet or meters (linear field), of the area you can see through a pair of binoculars is called the "field of view." In either case, the larger the field of view, the larger the area that appears in the image. A wide field of view is useful when observing things, such as birds or sports, that are likely to move; the narrower the field of view, the more often you will have to move and refocus the binoculars to keep the subject in view. Field of view is relative to magnification. The greater the magnification, the smaller the field of view usually is. Field of view is usually indicated on the body of the binoculars in degrees, feet, and meters. For example, the marking "8° 410 ft at 1000 yds" indicates that the field of view encompasses 8 degrees of an imaginary circle with you at the center; at 1,000 yards, the field of view is 410 feet wide. Birders prefer binoculars with as wide a field of view as possible without distortion at the edges. At the minimum, purchase binoculars with a field of view of at least 250 feet at 1,000 yards.

EXIT PUPIL

If you hold the binoculars at arm's length up to a light, you will see a small circle containing an image in the eyepiece. This circle is known as the "exit pupil." In general, the bigger the exit pupil, the brighter the image. Optimally, its diameter should match the maximum size that the pupil of your eye can dilate (widen) to under the lighting conditions you are most likely to encounter. If the exit pupil is the same size as your pupil, all the light transmitted by the binoculars enters your eye, and you get a bright image. If the exit pupil is larger than your pupil, some of the light falls on the iris and is wasted. If the exit pupil is smaller than your pupil, you may have difficulty keeping the image centered in your eye.

Under very dim conditions, the eye's pupil can open to a diameter no wider than about ¼ inch (7 millimeters). Thus, binoculars that would be useful for observations in early dawn or twilight conditions would have an exit pupil that size; with an exit pupil of only ⅛ or ³⁄₁₆ inch (4 to 5 mm), the binoculars would be useful only in full daylight. However, the eye's ability to dilate decreases with age. For middle-aged and older people, some of the light coming through the eyepiece may fall outside the pupil of the eye and not be perceived.

Because your pupils contract in bright light, binoculars with bigger objectives that gather more light will be no brighter when birdwatching on a sunny beach, for example, than binoculars with smaller objectives and the same magnification. If, on the other hand, you do a lot of your birding in shady woods or in twilight, a bigger exit pupil will be a definite asset. Bigger exit pupils are also helpful when you are birding from a moving platform—a boat, for example—because the larger exit pupil is easier to keep centered over your own pupil. As a rule, you will have more flexibility if you select binoculars with a bigger exit pupil.

Important as it is, the exit pupil number is not marked on binoculars. Check the descriptive specifications provided by the manufacturer.

The appearance of the exit pupil also lets you assess the quality of the prisms. All binoculars use prisms to orient the image correctly; otherwise, you would see things upside down through the binoculars. Look carefully at the shape of the exit pupil. In the best binoculars, the exit pupils are perfect circles centered in the eyepiece, indicating high-quality prisms accurately aligned. In lesser binoculars, the prisms can produce exit pupils that are elongated or off center or have the edges cut off, making them look like square pegs in round holes. The result is dim, distorted, or vignetted images. (See following for more about prisms.)

Transmittance

Transmittance is the amount of light that exits the binoculars and enters your eyes. A certain amount of light is lost through absorptions and reflection as the light passes through the complex arrangement of glass in the binoculars. The better the binoculars, the less light is lost; good modern binoculars transmit 90 percent or more of the light. The less the light loss, the brighter and thus more accurate and detailed the image.

Twilight factor

The twilight factor is a more useful relative measure of brightness, especially for birders, who are often observing under less than full daylight conditions. This factor measures both viewing efficiency and image detail in twilight conditions. To calculate the factor, multiply the magnification by the diameter of the objective in millimeters and then find the square root of the product. The larger the factor, the more efficient the binoculars are in dim light. For example, 8 x 32 binoculars would have a twilight factor of 16, whereas 20 x 80 binoculars would have a twilight factor of 40. The 20 x 80 binoculars would thus be better for dim light conditions, even though both might have exit pupils of the same size. For dim light, a twilight factor of at least 20 is recommended. Fortunately, the twilight factor is usually listed in the product literature, so you don't have to calculate it yourself.

Close focus

The closest distance at which the binoculars can focus is called the "close" or "near focus." Generally, the more powerful the binoculars, the farther the focus distance. Although much birding takes place at a distance, close focus of 10 feet or less is a valuable aspect for binoculars. Birders do sometimes get that close to a bird, but they're more likely to want close focus for watching butterflies, dragonflies, frogs, and other animal life. Most high-quality binoculars focus down to at least 7 feet;

some go as close as 3 feet, another good reason to spend the money for outstanding optics.

Eye relief

The distance between the outer surface of the eyepiece lens and the surface of your eye is called the "eye relief." Because the surface of your eye can't actually touch the surface of the lens, eye relief can make a difference in how much of the field of view you can see. To grasp this concept, imagine peeking through a keyhole. The closer your eye is to the opening, the more of the room inside you can see. In binoculars, the longer the eye relief, the farther away your eye can be from the eyepiece and still get a full view of the field.

Long eye relief is generally useful so that you don't have to hold the binoculars so close to your eyes that your eyelashes get in the way. It is particularly important if you wear eyeglasses all the time. The lenses in your eyeglasses keep you from bringing the eyepieces close to the surface of your eye; long eye relief lets you see most of the field of view anyway.

The eye relief is listed in millimeters in the manufacturer's literature. Long eye relief ranges from 15 to 20 millimeters; medium eye relief is between 8 and 15 millimeters. As a general guideline, look for the longest eye relief you can find within your price range.

The eyepieces of binoculars have soft rubber eye cups on them. If you don't wear eyeglasses, the eye cups are useful for blocking distracting extraneous light from entering your eyes while you look through the binoculars. If you wear eyeglasses, eye cups simply make the eye relief longer than is desirable. In either case, if necessary roll the cups down either partway or all the way to get the eye relief that suits you best.

PRISMS

Prisms are essential to binoculars, which may explain why the terminology is never really explained in the manufacturer's literature. In optics, prisms are used to change the direction of the light path through the use of internal reflection (as near total as possible). Two types of prisms commonly are used in binoculars: porro prisms (named for their inventor) and roof prisms (so called because they resemble pitched roofs). Binoculars made with porro prisms have the objective lenses farther apart than the eyepieces—the barrels of the binocular are offset from the eyepiece. In roof prism binoculars, the objective lenses and the eyepieces are in a straight line, giving the binoculars a streamlined look and making them easier to hold. Because they have fewer internal parts, roof prism binoculars are also very durable. They're also more expensive.

COATINGS

As light passes through the various optical elements that make up a pair of binoculars, it can be reflected around, leading to fuzzy, hazy, and low-contrast images. In addition, each element transmits slightly less than the light that hits it, leading to dim images. Optical coatings improve light transmission and reduce internal reflections.

Good binoculars are coated on all sides of all optical elements, with multiple antireflective coatings on all air-to-glass surfaces. Lousy binoculars are coated only on the outer objective and the outer eyepiece because these are the only parts you can see without taking the binoculars apart. Choose only binoculars with fully multicoated lenses.

PHASE CORRECTION

For complex reasons, the design of roof prism binoculars means that the light beams from each barrel can interfere with each other and get out of phase, leading to loss of contrast, resolution, and color accuracy. High-quality roof prism binoculars have antiphase-shifting coatings that correct this problem and give excellent color fidelity. Phase correction isn't an issue with porro prism binocs.

PURGING

To prevent internal fogging and oxidation and to keep out dust and debris, the normal air and moisture inside all good modern binoculars are removed and replaced with nitrogen or argon gas. The process is called "purging."

ARMORING

Birders should invest only in binoculars with armor coating. The advantages are many. Armored binoculars are quieter (they don't make noise and spook the birds when accidentally banged against a canteen, for example), don't produce glare or reflections, and are very sturdy. They are water resistant; in fact, many armored binoculars claim to be waterproof. (Don't test this claim if you can help it.) They are also easier to hold, especially when conditions are wet or cold.

Binocular sizes

Standard high-quality binoculars weigh anywhere from about nineteen ounces to about thirty-two ounces. Most modern 8 x 42s come in at around twenty-eight ounces. All other features being equal, choose the lightest binocs you can. A few ounces will start to matter on a long day in the field.

Compact binoculars usually weigh in at around seven to twelve ounces. Compacts are particularly handy for occasions when weight matters and birding is not the top priority—hikes, bike rides, and theatrical events. They also fit very conveniently into the glove box of a car and are handy for emergency birdwatching situations. Avoid zoom binoculars—they are heavy, clumsy, and dim and have overall inferior optics. You will definitely not see more birds with them.

Neck straps and other accessories

The purchase price of binoculars includes the neck strap, carrying case, and lens caps. (Beware of retailers who "strip" these accessories from the package and sell them separately.) Try out the neck strap on a field trip; if it feels as if it is cutting a permanent groove into your neck or shoulder, shop around for a strap that's more comfortable for you. Check the strap often and replace it immediately if it starts to show signs of wear, especially where it connects to the binoculars.

Various straps and harnesses meant to keep binoculars from weighing down your neck and bouncing on your chest are available. They work reasonably well. A significant drawback is that you must disentangle yourself from them every time you want to take off or put on a layer of clothing.

Tripod adapters allow the binoculars to be mounted on a standard tripod for more stable, vibration-free viewing. The adapters aren't universal; consider buying the appropriate adapter when you purchase the binoculars just to have it on hand should you need it.

Using Binoculars

Using your binoculars is very simple, although it does take a bit of practice to get the most out of them. Learn to use the features that follow.

Interpupillary distance

"Interpupillary distance" is an elaborate way of saying the space between your eyes or, more specifically, the space between the pupils. This distance varies from person to person, which is why binoculars have a central hinge connecting the two halves. Look through the binoculars and move the two halves together or apart until you see one clear circle of image.

Focusing

Focus the binoculars by looking through them and using your index finger to rotate the central focusing ring found on the body hinge. Rotate to the right to focus farther in; rotate to the left to focus farther out. Porro prism binoculars focus by moving the eyepieces in and out; roof prism binoculars focus internally. When selecting new binoculars, make sure you can reach the focusing ring easily without shifting your grip on the binoculars.

Diopter focus

Most people, even those with very good eyesight, see slightly better through their right eye. To accommodate the difference, a diopter (standard unit of optical measurement) adjustment mechanism is built into the right eyepiece. To adjust it, first use both eyes to focus the binoculars on something with sharp edges not too far away—a sign, for example. Close your left eye and look only through the right eyepiece. If the image is slightly out of focus, rotate the diopter adjustment until the image is sharp. Note the degree of correction by looking at the diopter or plus and minus markings on the right eyepiece. After you have set the diopter adjustment, it stays set—you don't have to change it when you change the central focus.

Fatigue

A few hours of keeping your arms raised while holding up your binoculars will lead to fatigue, trembling arms, and sometimes muscle cramps in the hands. Tired arms will also exaggerate the normal amount of shake transmitted to the binoculars from your body. Lighter binoculars sometimes help, but the fatigue really comes from the weight of your arms, not your binoculars. You can try propping your elbows on something— a handy fencepost—but this will exaggerate body shake. For extended viewing of a specific spot such as a nest, a tripod is a good idea.

Eye fatigue is a big problem for birders and can lead to nasty headaches. The best way to reduce eye fatigue is to use good binoculars to begin with. Remember to use the diopter adjustment. Wear polarized sunglasses on bright days. *Caution!*

Never look at the sun through binoculars! Serious eye damage can result!

Eyeglasses

If you wear eyeglasses only sometimes—just for reading or driving—or if you wear bifocals, should you keep them on or off while using binoculars? It's probably best to keep them on. You don't want to be caught fumbling around with your glasses when a good bird flies by. You also don't want to drop or lose them. If you wear prescription eyeglasses, make sure the prescription is accurate.

Caring for binoculars

Binoculars, especially if they are armored, are surprisingly sturdy. This does not mean, however, that they can be dropped, soaked, or otherwise abused with impunity. The best way to avoid disaster is always to keep the strap around your neck or over your shoulder. Some high-quality binoculars now come with built-in, flip-up lens caps for the eyepieces. This is very helpful for keeping the eyepieces dry on wet days. Traditional individual eyepiece covers are more trouble than they are worth in the field. Put them on, along with the objective covers, when you store the binoculars. The carrying case is handy if you are packing the binoculars in a suitcase for a long trip; otherwise, forget about it. Birders always want their binoculars to be where they can get at them immediately. Water and mud should be gently wiped away with a soft cloth. Use lens cleaning fluid on the objectives and eyepieces. Never place the fluid directly on the lens. Instead, place a drop or two on a microwoven cleaning cloth. Lens cleaning fluid and cleaning cloths are easily available at any drugstore.

Binoculars do occasionally get damaged by being dropped or soaked. Lenses and internal optical elements can be cracked, broken, knocked out of alignment, or damaged by water (especially salt water). Even the best binoculars are not totally immune to the effects of moisture and dust. If repair or cleaning is needed, contact the manufacturer to get more information and to find authorized service centers. If the binoculars have been dunked, do this immediately to minimize further damage to the coatings.

BUYING BINOCULARS

Most camera and department stores carry binoculars; numerous excellent Web sites also sell optics, often with an excellent selection at very competitive prices. For the best selection, service, and price, shopping online with a reputable company such as EagleOptics.com is the way to go. The drawback is that you don't get to handle the binoculars and decide which feels most comfortable for you. To get around this, look at as many models as you can by trying the binoculars of as many of your birding friends (and even complete strangers) as possible. Read the reviews of binoculars that appear in the birding magazines and Web sites. Check out the specs at the manufacturers' Web sites.

After you've purchased your binoculars, register the warranty, make a note of the serial number, and save the receipt and any other documentation. Mark the binoculars with your name in an indelible manner.

SPOTTING SCOPES

After a few frustrating birding trips using binoculars to try to distinguish among the assorted shorebirds huddled on a distant mud flat, you will want to own a spotting scope or become very good friends with someone who does.

Essentially a compact, portable, and powerful telescope, a spotting scope is an invaluable tool for birding. Beyond about 100 feet, binoculars can't provide distinguishing details. With a spotting scope, you pick out fine details, observe distant behavior and nests up to 200 yards away, and even seen the moons of Jupiter. By adding a camera adapter, spotting scopes become powerful telephoto lenses for photography and videography. A spotting scope is considerably more expensive than an excellent pair of binoculars, but the new dimensions it will bring to your birding make it worth every penny and then some.

Much of the terminology used to describe spotting scopes, such as "exit pupil" and "twilight factor," is the same as that for binoculars, but there are some differences. The objective lenses are in a long, offset barrel; the body contains the focusing knob, the erecting prism (otherwise the image would be upside down), and the eyepiece. Imagine one side of a pair of very large porro prism binoculars, and you are visualizing a spotting scope.

APERTURE

The diameter of the objective lens, expressed in millimeters, is the aperture of a spotting scope. As with binoculars, the bigger the aperture, the brighter and more detailed the image.

Generally speaking, spotting scopes for nature study have apertures ranging from 65 to 80 millimeters.

Magnification

Two factors determine the magnification of a spotting scope: the objective lens and the eyepiece. Magnification is determined by dividing the focal length of the objective lens by the focal length of the eyepiece. A good rule of thumb is that the useful (not theoretical) magnification of a spotting scope is about two-thirds of the aperture. For example, a 60-millimeter scope would have a magnification of about 40x. For most birding situations, 40x is more than adequate. As with binoculars, higher magnification means a narrower field of view and a dimmer image.

Exit pupil

Conceptually, the exit pupil on a spotting scope is the same as it is with binoculars. Realistically, the exit pupil on a scope is usually smaller. The higher the magnification, the smaller the exit pupil. To determine the size of the exit pupil with a particular eyepiece, divide the aperture by the magnification. A 60-millimeter aperture with a 30x eyepiece, for example, would have an exit pupil of 2 millimeters.

Eyepieces

The eyepiece of a spotting scope magnifies the primary image produced by the objective lenses. Needless to say, eyepieces are critical to good performance. They are usually sold separately, although one eyepiece may be part of the deal. Because different eyepieces are appropriate for different viewing conditions, you may want to purchase at least two. With a few exceptions, eyepieces from one manufacturer will not fit into scopes from another manufacturer.

Eyepieces come in various configurations: fixed, wide-angle, and zoom (also called "variable"). Fixed eyepieces come in magnifications ranging from 15x to 60x, with assorted intervals in between. Wide-angle eyepieces offer fewer magnification options; they are usually available in 20x, 30x, or 45x. Zoom eyepieces usually come in 15–45x or 20–60x magnifications. Zooms are flexible, but the field of view is generally narrower. In addition, the image is often less bright because it must pass through additional optical elements. As you zoom in, depth of field (the portion of the image that is in focus from front to back) diminishes, as does the exit pupil.

Eye relief is important when choosing eyepieces. The principles are exactly the same as for binoculars. The higher the magnification on the eyepiece, the less the eye relief—a problem for eyeglass wearers who want to work at high magnifications. The abbreviation "LER" in the manufacturer's literature means "long eye relief."

Eyepiece placement

The eyepiece on a spotting scope can be placed in a straight line with the objective or offset at a 45-degree angle. The placement makes no real difference to the optics, but it can affect your viewing comfort. Straight-through designs are easier to aim (just sight down the barrel), easier to use when mounted on a car window, and easier to use for photography. On the other hand, if you are tall, you will have to raise your tripod quite high to see through the scope comfortably. A tripod extended to its full length can be unstable, especially on uneven surfaces.

Offset eyepieces let you bend over at a comfortable angle to view the image. For extended viewing, this posture may be less of a strain on the back. Offset eyepieces also make it easier for several people of different heights to share the scope because the tripod height doesn't have to be constantly adjusted.

Twilight factor

The twilight factor in spotting scopes has the same importance as it does in binoculars.

Close focus

Spotting scopes are meant for observing at a distance. The closest near focus for a typical scope is generally about 16–20 feet. For anything closer, use your binoculars.

Using Spotting Scopes

Spotting scopes are most valuable for viewing where the landscape is fairly open and the birds are visible and relatively still—coastlines, tidal marshes, wetlands, and the like—or for observing fixed points such as nests. They are not very helpful for viewing in wooded areas or for tracking fast-moving birds.

Don't try to search for birds with the scope as if it were binoculars. Instead, use your binoculars to sweep the area and note the location of birds you want to study further. Set up the scope and tripod on as flat an area as you can, adjusting the legs as necessary to compensate for unevenness. Make sure the tripod is stable before doing anything else. In windy conditions, try to keep one hand on the tripod at all times.

Aiming the spotting scope can be difficult at first, especially if you use one with an offset eyepiece. To aim a straight-through scope, simply look down the outside of the barrel. To aim an offset scope, use the built-in device provided by the manufacturer. This could be a line-of-sight peep bar, a peep sight, or a notch-and-bead sight (also called an "iron sight") that runs parallel to the sighting axis of the scope. Look along or through the device and move the tripod head until the sight is directly on your target. When you look through the eyepiece, you should find the bird right in the center. With a little practice, you will be able to get the bird into your sights quickly every time.

On a typical birding trip, you will move the scope and tripod to a number of sites. You don't need to take the scope off the tripod every time you move on. Before picking the combination up, however, make sure the scope is snugly attached to the tripod head. If you are on foot, carrying the scope/tripod combination can be awkward (especially on narrow trails) and tiring. Try to avoid snagging vegetation and banging into trees and other people. Watch your footing. If you are driving from point to point, you will be moving the scope/tripod into and out of the car a lot. Try laying the combination across the back seat.

To help you set up your tripod quickly, extend the legs to the correct height for you and then mark the extension points on the legs with paint or waterproof ink.

Buying Spotting Scopes

As with binoculars, a spotting scope is a major purchase. Research the possibilities, try out as many as you can, then shop around online for the best price. Compared with binoculars, there are fewer manufacturers and options to choose from, so it's a little easier to make up your mind.

DIGISCOPING

The modern digital camera—simple point-and-shoot or complex DSLR—or video camera can be combined with a spotting scope to capture amazingly detailed and bright close-up shots. The key is an adapter that connects the camera to the scope. The details vary considerably among scope and camera brands. Because the exit pupil image coming through the scope (use a fixed-focus eyepiece) is small, often under 4 millimeters, the camera lens needs to be centered precisely. The adapter has to provide a firm connection between the scope eyepiece and the camera; it also has to move easily away from the eyepiece so you can move easily between looking through the scope and taking the picture. To avoid vibration, the camera or adapter should have a cable shutter release mechanism. A variety of well-designed adapters is now available for scopes. Which one is best for you will depend on both the scope and the camera. DSLR cameras work best for digiscoping if they have an optical zoom of 3x or 4x and at least five megapixels of resolution. On the other hand, in a birding emergency, such as documenting a rarity, a point-and-shoot or even cell phone camera can be held up to the scope eyepiece.

TRIPODS

For any viewing through a spotting scope, a tripod is a necessity. Spotting scopes magnify *everything*—including body vibrations and wind shake, and they are far too heavy to hold in your hand for long. If you've just spent a small fortune to buy the spotting scope of your dreams, get a good sturdy tripod to support it. Select a tripod that is solid, with as little wobble as possible. The heavier the tripod, the more it will damp out vibrations. You don't have to buy a monster heavy-duty model, but do select one that weighs at least three pounds. On the other hand, you'll be hauling the scope and tripod around in the field, so you want the lightest possible tripod. For the best combination of strength and weight, look for a lightweight tripod made using carbon fiber; these usually weigh in at 3.5–5 pounds. Different brands have different ways to adjust the leg height; most birders prefer quick-action lever locks.

The spotting scope connects to the tripod at the head, which is detachable and is often sold separately. Tripod heads allow you to pan and tilt the scope and then lock it into position. The pan/tilt handle is usually removable and can be positioned for left-handed or right-handed use. A quick-release system on the head is handy because it allows the scope to be attached and removed quickly and easily, even while you are wearing gloves.

When selecting a tripod, check its minimum and maximum heights. The maximum height is usually anywhere between 43 and 51 inches without the center column extended; with the column extended, the maximum height is usually in the range of 51 to 65 inches.

Tripod Accessories

You may want to invest in a tripod bag or case, especially if you plan to check the tripod through as baggage when you travel by plane. Sturdy tripod straps for carrying the assembled scope and tripod make hauling them around a lot easier.

Other Supports

Table-top tripods, also called "shooter's stands," are compact, sturdy, and rigid. They rarely rise much more than 16 inches. They are handy if you need to set up the scope on the hood or roof of your car, but you can easily live without them.

Monopods are basically adjustable poles with a pan head attached. They are much lighter than tripods but obviously are not as stable and can't be used for hands-free viewing. Use a monopod only with low-powered optics—there's too much vibration for anything high powered.

At times a tripod is just inconvenient—too heavy to carry on a long hike, too awkward on a boat, or too slow to adjust for fast-moving birds. Shoulder mounts are a good option in these circumstances. The spotting scope is mounted onto a lightweight adjustable frame with a handgrip at the front and a rifle-style shoulder stock at the rear. As with monopods, use shoulder mounts only with low-powered optics.

Window mounts are tripod heads attached to a clamp that fits over the top edge of your car window (you have to roll the window down at least halfway). Window mounts are great for times when the weather is really bad because you can sit comfortably in your car and still birdwatch.

9
BIRDING IN THE FIELD

You've grasped the basic concepts of field identification; you know where the birds are; your binocular lenses are sparkling. It's time to go birding.

FIELD TRIPS

As a beginner, you will spend a lot of time focusing excitedly on clumps of dead leaves, stubs of broken branches, rags and plastic shopping bags clinging to fences, old newspapers stuck in bushes, and quivering twigs from which a bird has just flown. Many of the warblers you see will turn into House Sparrows on closer inspection; the Peregrine Falcons will turn out to be Herring Gulls. This can be frustrating beyond description, particularly when you *know* that there are lots of good birds in the area because they are singing tauntingly all around you. Keep looking. To a degree, artistry in birding is achieved like artistry in anything else: practice, practice, practice.

And just as beginning (and even professional) musicians take lessons, birdwatchers learn from more experienced birders. By far the best way to get a good lesson in birding is to go on a bird walk or field trip with an experienced leader. You can do this easily in your own locale with your local bird club. You can also attend one of the many birding symposiums and workshops sponsored by birding organizations and regional tourism associations. The annual spring and autumn weekends sponsored by New Jersey Audubon at Cape May, for example, draw hundreds of friendly and enthusiastic birders from all over the country and even overseas. New birders are as welcome as old hands.

A good field trip leader combines encyclopedic natural history knowledge with good humor, patience, and a lucky streak. The leader's goal is to make sure that everyone on the trip sees as many birds as possible. Don't let diffidence hold you back. If everyone else has spotted the bird and you still haven't, say so—quietly and without a lot of arm waving. The leader and the rest of the group will make an extra effort to help you see it.

Often, when someone spots a bird, he or she will say helpfully, "It's in the top left part of that tree," while gesturing vaguely ahead. Amazing to the novice, all other members of the group immediately train their binoculars exactly on the bird. In fact, this happens because several people have sighted the bird simultaneously or because they already suspected there was something in that tree. If you still can't see the bird, look in the same general direction as everyone else while listening for further bulletins from the group. These take the shape of a continuing stream of behavior reports ("It's pecking at the branch" or "It's scratching its head"), movement reports ("It just hopped down a little" or the dreaded "It just flew"), identification reports ("Looks like a Gray-cheeked Thrush," countered by "Can't be; no eye ring; must be Swainson's"), and admiration ("Just look at the color on that Indigo Bunting!"). You will also hear at least one other member of the group announce that he or she can't see it. At this point, additional aiming bulletins begin. Birders often use the clock system to pinpoint a location, so the bulletin might be "It's at two o'clock in the hickory tree." Alternatively and less helpfully, the reference point might be a peculiarity of the spot, along the lines of "It's just to the left of that big splintered branch." Again, if you haven't spotted the bird yet, say so. Next come additional directions that lead you through a series of obvious reference points until you reach the bird: "See the gate? See the stump just to the left of it? Now look in the lower right branches of the small tree by the big rock about 20 feet to the left of the stump. Got it?" As a desperate last measure, pointing a finger or even yanking a head into a better viewpoint will be forthcoming. Eventually, the bird will fly off, and the group will move on to repeat the performance elsewhere. Sometimes the leader will stop at a likely spot and try to pish up a bird. Stand by quietly with binoculars at the ready and watch carefully for movement. Avoid pointing if you spot a bird—this tends to make it flush.

Field trips to wetlands areas with dike roads often take the form of caravans. Participants meet in the parking lot and form a line of cars that proceeds around the road, stopping at the turnouts. At each turnout, all members of the group pile out of the cars, set up their spotting scopes, and begin scanning. Because these areas are flat and open and tend to have monotonously similar vegetation (mostly phragmites), directions to a bird of interest can be even harder to follow, especially when they are expressed as "It's just to the right of the dowitcher." Fortunately, the leader will focus a spotting scope on the interesting birds and make sure everyone gets a good look.

An average field trip to a local birding area—one sponsored by your local bird club, for instance—gets under way between seven and eight o'clock in the morning. At the normal leisurely pace, the trip is over within two hours and covers no more than 2 miles of fairly easy walking. Field trips to see shorebirds tend to last longer because the birds are visible and active longer. Special excursions to hot spots can be all-day or even overnight trips because of the travel time involved.

As a trip participant, you should observe proper birding etiquette. Arrive on time for the start of the trip (although the trip is unlikely to start exactly on time). Leave dogs and young children home. Avoid doing anything that will frighten away or harm the birds—don't approach too closely, point, move abruptly, or speak loudly. If you see a bird, even if you can't identify it, alert the group, giving the most precise directions you can. Be careful not to step into anyone's line of vision, particularly if photography is going on. Stay with the group; don't get ahead of the leader. In a caravan, offer a ride to anyone who needs it and drive carefully. Share your spotting scope, your snacks, your tissues, and anything else. Be sure to thank the group leader at the end.

DRESSING FOR THE FIELD

Your birding field trip starts when you get dressed at home. What you wear can make all the difference to your trip's success. Dress properly, and you will have an enjoyable and productive excursion; dress improperly, and you will be miserable.

FOOTWEAR

Comfortable, broken-in footwear appropriate to the weather and terrain is essential to any birding trip. Birders do a lot of walking. You will very quickly regret wearing inappropriate, new, or ill-fitting shoes of any kind as your blisters rise and your spirits sink. For general birdwatching on ordinary trails, a comfortable pair of light hiking boots or walking shoes is usually sufficient. For more rugged terrain, heavier, ankle-high hiking boots may be in order.

Cold feet will quickly make you feel cold all over; cold, wet feet will have this effect even more quickly. In cold weather, wear warm socks, preferably made of wool or a wool blend. Wool has the significant advantage of retaining heat even when wet. A polypropylene liner sock is also a good idea. Insulated boots and shoes containing Thinsulate or the equivalent are lightweight and comfortable and really do keep your feet warm.

Waterproof footwear is particularly desirable in the spring, when the trails are most likely to be wet and muddy. Leather footwear can be successfully treated with water-proofing substances. Muddy trails and trails covered with wet, fallen leaves can be treacherously slick. Good traction from the soles of your footwear is as important as water resistance.

Most good hiking boots are water resistant at least to some degree, but solid rubber is the only material that really keeps the water out. Boots with rubber lowers and leather or synthetic uppers are effective. Another good choice is rub-ber Wellington boots worn with warm socks instead of—not over—shoes. A great advantage of Wellies is that they can be simply hosed off to get them clean.

Hats

It's a good idea to wear a hat while birding. In cold weather, a hat greatly reduces heat loss from your head and helps keep you warmer longer. Be sure the hat covers your ears—frostbitten ears are no fun. In hot weather, a hat shades your head and helps keep you cool. In all weather, a hat keeps your head dry.

Select a hat that is comfortable, appropriate to the weather, snugly fitting, and has a brim to shade your eyes and keep precipitation off your face (particularly important if you wear eyeglasses). Wear a baseball-style cap with a long brim for extra shading in very bright situations—beaches, for example.

Clothing

Sturdy, comfortable clothing appropriate to the weather and the terrain is essential for a field trip. Birding is hard on your clothes, especially trousers and outerwear. You will often get wet, muddy, or worse. Select clothing that can survive rough treatment.

Dress for the weather. This does not mean the weather where you are when you get dressed—it means the weather where you will be when you are birding. An overcast but mild spring day with a refreshing breeze in the city is likely to be light rain, chilly temperatures, and a biting wind at the coastal refuge you are visiting. Check in advance. Always dress in easily removed layers. It is far better to arrive at your destination and take off your sweater than it is to get there and be cold with no recourse.

Novice birders are often shockingly unprepared for cold weather. Invest in good thermal underwear, heavy socks, wool or flannel-lined trousers, warm sweaters or fleece, and a good hooded parka (preferably down filled). In moderately cold weather, you can get away with thin gloves that let you focus your binoculars while wearing them. It is almost impossible to focus your binocs wearing thick, clumsy ski-type gloves. In really cold weather, try wearing thin silk or fleece gloves underneath down-filled mittens. Slip your hand out of the mitten to focus.

As you bundle up for cold weather, be sure you can move your arms freely. A parka that binds every time you lift your binoculars becomes very annoying very quickly.

In hot weather, wear loose, lightweight clothing, preferably made of cotton. Avoid shorts and sandals.

In all weather, carry a lightweight wind/rain shell. Such a shell folds up into a small package that fits easily into a pocket or pack. A tip for birders with long hair: Bring a hair clip. Wind-whipped hair in the eyes will seriously diminish your birding pleasure.

To reduce the chances of spooking the birds, avoid white or brightly colored clothing, anything adorned with reflective material (sequins, metal studs, etc.), and anything that clanks (jewelry, metal water bottles, etc.). Go with muted, dark colors, earth tones, or even camouflage gear.

Birding vests

Birders like comfortable, efficient clothing with lots of big, easily accessible pockets. Several manufacturers make lightweight, sturdy birding vests that have pockets specifically designed to hold field guides, notebooks, checklists, pencils, cameras, tissues, cell phones, sandwiches, snacks, hats, water bottles, bird callers, and all the other essential paraphernalia of birding.

Birding vests can be warm on hot days, and they don't fit very well over parkas. They can also make you look a little dorky or cause you to be mistaken for a fly fisher—but you're a birder and don't care what people think. An adjunct or alternative to a birding vest is a hip pack or backpack. The larger sizes can easily accommodate a field guide and lunch with room to spare. Look for one with tie-down straps to carry a sweater or jacket.

Sunglasses

Glare from the sun is a big problem for birders because it reduces your perception of color and leads to eye fatigue and nasty headaches. High-quality polarized sunglasses are the obvious solution. If you wear prescription eyeglasses, get prescription sunglasses—snap-on sunglasses that cover your regular glasses can create annoying light reflections when you are using optics. They also add another layer of glass for the light to go through before it reaches your retina, leading to loss of brightness and accurate color perception.

A strap to hold your sunglasses or eyeglasses around your neck when you are not wearing them helps keep them from getting lost, although it may get entangled with your binoculars. Taking the slight risk of strangulation is preferable to losing an expensive pair of glasses. If you wear prescription eyeglasses all the time, consider using a retaining strap to hold them in place while you are on a birding excursion. Nothing will stop you from seeing birds faster than a lost or broken pair of eyeglasses.

Glare from water or snow and ice is as hard on your eyes as glare from a sandy beach on a summer afternoon. Bring your sunglasses along throughout the year.

OTHER ITEMS

With experience, you will develop your own assortment of useful odds and ends. You will, of course, be carrying a notebook, writing implement, and field guide. Plastic bags are handy for carrying botanical specimens and dead birds. They are also useful for protecting optics and other gear from water and dirt. Bring several. A large scrap of soft cloth or old towel is good for wiping off water and dirt from you and your equipment. A pocketknife is always a good tool to have. Always bring plenty of tissues—it may be a long way to the nearest restroom.

Cell phones, hand-held GPS units, iPods, digital cameras, and other electronic devices are valuable tools for birding. They are also noisy to the point of spooking birds and annoying fellow birders. Turn off phone ringers (use the vibrate feature) and mute (if possible) any features that make noise.

FOOD AND DRINK

Birding makes people hungry and thirsty. If you're planning an all-day trip, bring a hearty lunch and plenty of snacks such as fruit (fresh and dried), cookies, and pretzels. You may find yourself eating a frozen sandwich in the winter. Try carrying it in an insulated container or bring something warm (stew or chili, for example) in a Thermos instead. Don't forget a fork. In the summer, pack your food in an insulated container with ice packs to keep it cool and unspoiled. Even on a short trip, bring along some snacks.

Always bring something to drink. Plain tap water in a water bottle is the simplest and cheapest approach. Fruit juice and iced tea are also good. Avoid carbonated and alcoholic beverages—they will not quench your thirst. In cold weather, a Thermos of hot tea or coffee is essential. Drink plenty of fluids in both very hot *and* very cold weather.

Hazards to Birders

Birding is basically a safe activity with little likelihood of injury beyond the occasional blister or mosquito bite. The few minor hazards can be dealt with easily.

Insects

If you are bothered by insects and other creepy-crawlies—if an ant in the pantry sends you into a cleaning frenzy, if you panic at the sight of a spider, if you can't bear to pick up an earthworm—you will have a problem becoming a proficient birder. Birds like to go where the bugs are, and birders like to go where the birds are. Try to take a philosophical attitude toward bugs—think of them as bird food. And remember that there are 30 million insect species. You're outnumbered by billions to one.

Biting insects such as mosquitoes, gnats, chiggers, fire ants, black flies, greenhead flies, and ticks may be bird food, but they are also pests of the first order. At a minimum, anoint yourself and your clothing—particularly your socks and trouser legs—with plenty of insect repellent containing DEET before the start of your field trip. Learn to recognize and avoid fire ant mounds, wasp nests, and similar obvious dangers.

If you are so dedicated to birding as to venture onto a salt marsh in midsummer, no amount of insect repellent and protective clothing will keep you from being bitten by greenhead flies, mosquitoes, and other noxious insects. Even if you are less foolhardy, as a birder you must simply learn to live with a certain number of itchy bug bites.

Ticks, however, are another story. Birders are at serious risk from the nasty tick-borne illness Lyme disease, carried by the deer tick (*Ixodes scapularis*). Ticks are brown, eight-legged, wingless arthropods that feed on blood—human, mammal, and avian. Ticks climb into low, brushy vegetation in mixed grassland areas and wait for a potential host to brush by them. (Although it may seem as if they do, ticks do not jump onto hosts; they do not drop out of trees and bushes.) The tick then bites into the host to get a blood meal. After it has fed, the tick drops off. Generally, you won't feel a tick bite until after the tick is gone. At that point, the site may become red and itchy; then again, it may not.

Lyme disease has become the most common vector-borne disease in the United States; some 20,000 cases are reported every year. Lyme disease symptoms include a bull's-eye or solid red rash around or near the site of the bite (but only about half of all victims get the rash), chills and fever, headache, fatigue, stiff neck, muscle and joint pain, and swollen glands.

Although most tick bites are absolutely harmless, a bout with Lyme disease will seriously cut into your birdwatching.

Take no chances. Especially in the late spring and early summer, when ticks are most common, wear ankle-high footwear, long sleeves, long trousers, and a hat. Tuck your trouser ends into your socks, tuck your shirt into your trousers, and button your cuffs. Select light-colored clothing so ticks can be easily spotted. Stay on and to the center of trails and avoid brushing against vegetation at the edges. Don't go into brushy or grassy areas without trails. Use plenty of insect repellent, particularly around the ankles.

If you have been in an area where ticks are prevalent, check your body and clothing carefully afterward. Hairy areas of the body, especially the head, are very attractive to ticks. Ticks found crawling on the skin or clothing should simply be removed before they can attach themselves. There is no risk here—the tick must embed itself before it can transmit the disease. If a tick does attach itself, remove it promptly. Use a pair of tweezers to grasp the tick on either side of the head, as close to the skin as possible. Pull gently but steadily to remove the tick. Apply antiseptic to the bite site and wash your hands thoroughly. Make a note of the date. Early symptoms of Lyme disease usually appear within three to thirty days after the bite of an infected tick.

SUNBURN

You can get sunburn while birding even on a cool day in early spring or late autumn. Use sunscreen of the appropriate sun protection factor (SPF) for your skin. Apply your bug spray on top of the sunscreen. Be sure to put sunscreen on the back of your neck and hands. If you have a bald spot, cover it with a hat.

Poison ivy and other noxious plants

It's almost impossible to avoid poison ivy, poison oak, and poison sumac if you're a birder. Poison ivy, in particular, is ubiquitous. Poison oak is a little less common, and poison sumac is generally found only in swampy areas in the eastern and southern United States. Only about half of all people who come into contact with these plants will develop an itchy, oozy rash—but you won't know which half you're in until it happens to you.

An old adage for avoiding poison ivy is "Leaves of three, let it be." Poison ivy plants can be vines or shrubs. They have green, glossy, lobe-shaped leaves arranged in clusters of three. In the autumn, you will see clusters of small, white berries under the leaves—an important food source for birds. Don't touch. All parts of poison ivy, poison oak, and poison sumac plants, even if dead, contain the oily resin that causes irritation. Poison oak plants are bushy, with leaves that grow in clusters of three. The leaves have indentations that make them resemble oak leaves. Poison sumac is a woody shrub or small tree. The leaflets grow in pairs along a stalk. Learn to recognize and avoid these plants.

Hypothermia and frostbite

Birders, especially young children and older birders, are subject to hypothermia and frostbite because they may spend long periods of time outdoors in very cold weather—during a Christmas bird count, for example. Hypothermia is a dangerous and sometimes fatal condition caused by a drop in body temperature of more than 4 degrees F (2 degrees C).

Prolonged exposure to cold and windy weather, especially if you are improperly dressed, is a good way to bring on hypothermia; so is getting wet, even if you are properly dressed.

In frostbite, the skin and tissues beneath the skin have frozen. Your ears, hands, nose, and feet are most likely to become frostbitten.

Hypothermia and frostbite are serious medical conditions requiring prompt attention. The symptoms and treatment are described in any good first aid manual.

Heat exhaustion

If you spend a prolonged period outdoors in very hot weather and sweat heavily, heat exhaustion can occur. If untreated, heat exhaustion can lead to the much more serious—even life-threatening—condition known as "heatstroke" (sunstroke). Heatstroke requires emergency medical help. Study a first aid manual to learn the symptoms and treatment for heat-related conditions.

Lightning and severe weather

A sudden thunderstorm while you are visiting a beach, meadow, or other open area such as a golf course exposes you to the risk of a lightning strike. Head quickly for shelter if the sky begins to darken ominously, if you hear distant thunder, or if you see lightning. Do not take shelter under a tree! Your car, however, is a safe spot if you can't get indoors. Lightning storms can be accompanied by dangerous hail. Take shelter. Heavy downpours can lead to flash floods and local flooding. Take commonsense precautions: Don't wade or drive into a stream or puddle if you can't see its bottom, and don't drive onto flooded bridges.

Deer and the hunting season

Deer and birders tend to be active at the same times in the same places. This makes hitting a deer with your car a real possibility, especially at dawn or at dusk. If you see a deer on or near the road, stop if you can and wait for it to cross the road to go back into the woods. Where there is one deer, there are usually more. Wait at least a minute or two to see if any more come along.

Birders often feel antagonistic toward hunters, particularly waterfowl hunters. It's an understandable feeling but one based on ignorance. Hunters and fishers have been and remain a major force behind the conservation movement. Hunting and fishing organizations have done a great deal to help preserve and restore wetlands—a good example is Ducks Unlimited's work restoring grassland, wetlands, and forested areas and holding conservation easements on working farms, ranches, timberlands, and recreational lands across the country. In addition, licensing fees and duck stamp money are earmarked for conservation purposes. (Many birders also purchase duck stamps every year. These collectible items feature beautiful bird art.)

The real problem is that birders and hunters share the same territory—and that can be dangerous. During the hunting season, try to stick to places where hunting is forbidden. If you really must go into an area that may have hunters, don't wear your cammies. Adorn yourself with blaze orange, stick to the trails, and make noise. During the Wild Turkey season, never try to follow a turkey's call to its source. There's a good chance that what you are hearing is actually a hunter luring in a bird. You could be mistaken for a turkey, with tragic consequences.

PERSONAL SECURITY

As a group, birders are amazingly honest and generous. Whenever they find lost binoculars, cameras, field guides, even caps and gloves, they make a strenuous effort to get them back to their rightful owners. It is unlikely in the extreme that a birder would ever steal something from you. Birders, alas, are in the minority. Take some basic security precautions for yourself and your gear. Always lock your car and put the key in a secure pocket, preferably one with a buttoned flap, along with your wallet. Avoid leaving optics or their telltale cases in full view in the car. Put them into the trunk or under a seat or toss a blanket over them. Take appropriate measures for your personal security and remember that your cell phone may not work at a remote birding site.

10

FURTHER ADVENTURES IN BIRDING

When you become a birder, you become part of a well-organized network of like-minded individuals. Your opportunities to venture farther afield with your fellow birders are wide.

BIRDING ORGANIZATIONS

Three organizations are particularly important to birdwatchers: the National Audubon Society (NAS), the American Birding Association (ABA), and the Cornell Laboratory of Ornithology. A number of states also have active, independent Audubon societies.

A conservation organization with more than 550,000 members, the National Audubon Society works toward the preservation and wise use of America's natural heritage. The society's roots go back to 1886, when George Bird Grinnell, editor of the magazine *Forest and Stream,* formed the first American bird association, the Audubon Society, to protest the wholesale slaughter of birds by market gunners for their meat and plumes. The organization he founded became the National Audubon Society in 1940.

The National Audubon Society today has more than five hundred chapters and offices in thirty states; it also staffs ten regional offices and a public-policy office in Washington, D.C.

(see Appendix B). Its national sanctuary system has 150 units and protects more than 250,000 acres; hundreds of additional acres are protected by local chapters. Forty-five Audubon nature centers are located around the country, including in urban areas such as East Los Angeles. The National Audubon Society publishes the general nature magazine *Audubon.*

The National Audubon Society also has local chapters in just about every state, including those with independent Audubon societies (see following). To find a chapter near you and to learn more about NAS activities and services for birders, check the Web site at audubon.org.

A number of states have independent Audubon organizations not affiliated with the National Audubon Society. This confusing situation dates back to the start of the Audubon movement at the turn of the twentieth century, when numerous conservation organizations sprang up using the Audubon name. Many eventually coalesced into what is now the National Audubon Society, but some remained unaffiliated as state societies with their own local chapters, magazines, sanctuaries, and activities. To complicate matters further, the National Audubon Society has chapters in every state, including those with independent Audubons. Fortunately, peaceful coexistence and frequent cooperation seem to be the rule. Independent Audubons publish magazines and newsletters and sponsor field trips, lectures, birdathons, birding trips, and other activities. If you live in a state with an independent Audubon, join it (see Appendix B for details).

The American Birding Association is a birding-only organization founded in 1969. Many, but by no means all, ABA members are dedicated birders with a serious interest in listing and traveling to see birds; most members are recreational birders. The ABA is the semiofficial arbiter of birding records, tracking and publishing listing records, Big Day and Big Year reports, and other individual and group listing activities, and assessing rare-bird reports. The association publishes *Birding,* a bimonthly magazine with great photography and enjoyable articles on all aspects of birding, and the lively monthly newsletter *Winging It.* The scholarly journal *North American Birds* focuses on bird records. Each quarterly issue contains thirty-four regional reports, organized taxonomically and written by North America's top birders. The ABA sponsors conferences, conventions, workshops, and numerous birding trips throughout the year. The Web site at aba.org is an excellent way to track down upcoming birding festivals and other events and to find local birding clubs. A major advantage of joining the ABA is receiving member discounts on the very wide selection of high-quality optics and birding books, including finding guides for virtually everywhere, that is carried in the sales catalog.

The Cornell Laboratory of Ornithology in Ithaca, New York, was founded in 1955. The lab conducts a number of citizen science research projects, such as Project FeederWatch and the Great Backyard Bird Count (see chapter 3), and sponsors the outstanding All About Birds Web site. Membership in the lab brings you discounts on the very broad selection of books, recordings, and other bird-related materials and gifts from the lab's online birding shop, along with a subscription to the stunning quarterly magazine *Living Bird* and the *BirdScope* newsletter.

Birders with Disabilities

A physical disability is no handicap to birdwatching. Today most public nature areas—parks, campgrounds, and wildlife sanctuaries—are fully accessible to wheelchairs, with ramps, wider doors, restroom facilities, paved nature walks and viewing areas, and other facilities. Many parks now have water access and even wheelchair fishing areas—excellent places for seeing shore and water birds.

At many of the best birdwatching sites, a mobility handicap is hardly a problem at all. For instance, the best way to bird many wetlands sanctuaries is to drive along the dike road. You can easily see numerous birds without ever getting out of the car, especially if you use a window-mounted spotting scope. The hawkwatching site at Cape May Point is right next to a large, flat, paved parking lot, making it easily accessible.

Additional Reading

Your field guide is just the first of many birding books you will soon begin to accumulate.

Two useful books are good basic introductions to birding: *Sibley's Birding Basics* by David Sibley and *National Geographic Birding Essentials* by Jonathan Alderfer and Jon L. Dunn.

For more detail about birds in general, invest in some of the standard, up-to-date reference works. A good general book is *Lives of North American Birds* by Kenn Kaufman. The *Firefly New Encyclopedia of Birds,* edited by Chris Perkins, is beautifully illustrated with hundreds of great photos.

For practical birdwatching, a must-have book is *The Birder's Handbook* by Paul Ehrlich, David Dobkin, and Darryl

Wheye. This book bills itself very accurately as "the essential companion to your identifications guide." Also in the must-have category is *The Sibley Guide to Bird Life and Behavior,* written and illustrated by David Sibley. The three-volume *Audubon Society Master Guide to Birding,* now out of print, is valuable for its detailed discussion and illustration of field marks.

In a category by itself is Christopher Leahy's witty and informative book, *The Birdwatcher's Companion.* This volume contains, in encyclopedia form, entries on virtually every aspect of birds and birdwatching in North America. An enjoyable and instructive book full of useful tips is *Pete Dunne's Essential Field Guide Companion* by none other than Pete Dunne. *A World of Watchers* by Joseph Kastner and *Of a Feather: A Brief History of American Birding* by Scott Weidensaul put birding into historical perspective. A very enjoyable book is *Whose Bird?* by Bo Boelens and Michael Watkins. This title looks at common bird names and the people they commemorate.

When you think you're ready to take on the challenges of gull identification and other complicated issues, *Peterson Field Guide to Advanced Birding* by Kenn Kaufman will be your bible.

If you are interested in feeding and attracting birds, read *The Audubon Society Guide to Attracting Birds* by Stephen W. Kress. To understand the behavior of your backyard birds, see the guides to bird behavior by Donald and Lillian Stokes.

The mysteries of bird migration are covered in *How Birds Migrate* by Paul Kerlinger and *Living on the Wind* by Scott Weidensaul.

Every year numerous books about the joys of birds and birdwatching are published. When you can't go birding yourself, the next-best activity is reading about it. The classic works of naturalists such as Aldo Leopold, Alexander Skutch, Peter Matthiessen, and Niko Tinbergen are still enjoyable and valuable today. The birding adventures of contemporary writers such as Pete Dunne, Tim Gallagher, and Kenn Kaufman and the extensive subgenre of birding quests (Big Years, rarities, and so on) make entertaining reading, especially on long winter evenings.

Birders inevitably accumulate assorted field guides on other aspects of natural history—rocks, wildflowers, trees, fungi, butterflies and moths, and bugs of every description. To learn about butterflies, *Butterflies through Binoculars* by Jeffrey Glassberg, in east and west volumes, is an excellent starting point. For dragonflies, try *Dragonflies through Binoculars* by Sidney W. Dunkle.

MAGAZINES AND JOURNALS

The articles in birding and natural history magazines are an excellent way to learn more about birds. Magazines such as *BirdWatcher's Digest, Birder's World, Birds & Blooms,* and *Wild-Bird* carry interesting, entertaining, illustrated articles that are full of solid information without being too technical. *Birder's World,* in particular, features outstanding color photography. *Birding, North American Birds,* and *Living Bird* are more technical but still very accessible.

The ornithological journals such as *The Auk, Condor,* and *Wilson Bulletin* are much more serious. Don't be intimidated. You may not understand every nuance of the statistical data in an article, but you can certainly grasp the main points.

Local, state, provincial, and regional birding clubs and organizations all publish newsletters and magazines. A subscription is usually part of the membership fee. You, too, can experience the joys of authorship by writing an article for your bird club's newsletter.

For more information about birding magazines, see Appendix C.

Bird Photography

Many birders are also serious photographers. They take pictures for a broad spectrum of reasons, but for many, the primary purpose is to capture the beauty of the birds. This is a very old impulse in humans—depictions of recognizable bird species have been found in Paleolithic cave paintings that are nearly 20,000 years old.

For beginners, photographs taken in the field can be a helpful tool for identification and documentation as well as being an introduction to an absorbing aspect of birdwatching. To take even a minimally acceptable picture of a bird, you will need a good 35-millimeter digital single-lens reflex camera, a telephoto lens (at least 120 millimeters) or spotting scope with digital camera adapter, and as many memory cards as possible.

If you are photographing the bird simply to have a record of it, or if you are documenting a rarity, do your best to take a good picture without worrying too much about artistic merit. Try to make the photo sharply focused, well lit, and properly exposed, but, if that's not possible, just do the best you can. Even a poor photo is better than no picture at all, particularly when it comes to documenting rarities. If the bird cooperates, try to get as many shots as possible, concentrating on the field marks. If you can, try to get a shot that shows the bird near something that provides a natural scale for size comparison.

You will often encounter bird photographers at birding sites and on field trips. Be courteous. Don't stand or set up your scope in front of their camera. Stay away from a blind if you know it is occupied by a photographer. Above all, don't do anything that will flush the bird.

Serious bird photography as an art and science is far too complex for the scope of this volume. Some excellent books on the subject are *Nature Photography: Insider Secrets from the World's Top Digital Photography Professionals* by Chris Weston, *Art of Bird Photography* by Arthur Morris, *National Audubon Society Guide to Nature Photography: Digital Edition* by Tim Fitzharris, and *John Shaw's Nature Photography Field Guide* by John Shaw.

Recording Bird Sounds

Recent advances in recording equipment have made it easier for birders to make their own recordings of bird sounds. The gear has become much lighter and easier to use. It has also become less expensive, but it is not by any means cheap. At a minimum, recording requires a high-quality parabolic or shotgun microphone, headphones, a high-quality digital audio recorder, and audio editing software. This minimum package could easily cost you well over a thousand dollars. A fairly high level of expertise is needed to use the equipment and software effectively. Despite the cost and complexity, this is a rapidly growing area of interest for many birders. How-to articles and product reviews appear often in the popular birding magazines. Another good source of information is the Web site of the Macaulay Library of Natural Sounds at the Cornell Laboratory of Ornithology at macaulaylibrary.org. The library houses the world's largest collection of bird and animal sounds, contributed by amateurs and professionals from all around the world.

HURT BIRDS

As you watch birds, you may encounter birds that are sick or injured. You may also encounter damaged nests and "abandoned" chicks. What should you do?

In the case of sick and injured birds, the answer almost always is to leave the bird alone and let nature take its course. Don't allow human notions of compassion to interfere with the great web of life—and death. As discussed elsewhere, it is against federal law to keep any protected bird in captivity or to treat it unless you are a wildlife rehabilitator licensed by the federal government and state authorities.

One possible exception to the rule of noninterference is when a large bird such as a hawk or owl is injured—hit by a car, for example. These birds can sometimes be treated successfully and returned to the wild. Unfortunately, far more often they cannot be fully rehabilitated and must either be humanely destroyed or kept in captivity.

A number of wildlife rehabilitation centers have been established in North America. To find one near you, contact the International Wildlife Rehabilitation Council at iwrc-online.org.

Sometimes a nest full of eggs or chicks will fall out of a tree, usually after a period of high winds. If you find such a nest, simply place it back into the tree, tying it in place with string if necessary. If you don't know which tree it came from, just pick a good spot in any nearby tree; the parent birds will find the nest.

Sometimes you will find an unfledged chick that has fallen out of the nest. If you can find the nest, simply place the chick back into it; if not, place the chick on a low branch as close to where you found it as possible. Birds have virtually no sense of smell, and the idea that a bird will abandon its young if it smells humans on them has no basis in fact. It is unadvisable and probably unnecessary to take the chick in and raise it yourself. This is an extremely demanding task that is almost certain to end in heartbreak and failure. A certain amount of unsuccessful nesting is a sad but normal part of avian ecology. Ornithologists estimate that, on average, only one nest in ten is completely successful.

Every now and then, you, or more likely your young child, will come across a baby bird that appears to be abandoned. However, the bird almost certainly has not been abandoned. Many birds leave the nest before they are fully fledged; the parent birds continue to feed and care for them. In all probability, a parent of the "abandoned" bird is nearby, waiting for you to leave. If you move away a few yards and quietly wait, you will hear the parent calling to the chick and its answering peeps. Keep watching, and you may be rewarded and relieved by seeing the parent feed the chick.

Birdathons and Big Days

Birdathons are competitive birding events generally held between April 1 and May 30, depending on the peak spring migration at the particular locales. Sponsors pledge money for each bird that a birdwatching team spots during the chosen twenty-four-hour period; participants also compete for awards and donated prizes. The proceeds are used to help finance local birding projects and sanctuaries. The annual World Series of Birding, sponsored by New Jersey Audubon every spring, is probably the best-known birdathon, garnering extensive media coverage. Needless to say, the logistics and execution of a twenty-four-hour birding expedition by a five-person team are exhaustive and exhausting.

Big Days also occur during the peak spring migration period, with the date varying according to locale. Participants in a Big Day try to see as many species as possible in a twenty-four-hour period, but they are free to travel as widely as they wish within the period (aircraft may be used). Big Days are often organized by a group of birding friends or by local bird clubs; they are more local and informal than birdathons. Serious birders report their totals to the American Birding Association.

Individual birders can challenge themselves to do a Big Year (the less ambitious settle for Big Weeks or Big Months), in which they attempt to see as many birds as possible in a defined area, usually a state, a region, or all of North America. A certain amount of disdain for the ordinary working world is necessary for this sort of activity. The people who do it have a lot of exhausting fun and often contribute to birding knowledge by discovering previously undocumented species or breeding sites.

Beginning birders are sometimes intimidated by organized counting events. After all, the people who do them see more birds in a day than many beginners have on their life lists. The publicity given to some counts tends to give a distorted picture of birding, putting the emphasis on quantity, not quality. If you can, participate in a count. You'll contribute to a worthy cause, add to scientific knowledge, expand your birding horizons, and generally have a ton of fun.

BIRDING EDUCATION

Formal—but fun—instruction in birdwatching and ornithology is available through summer and vacation birding programs sponsored by a variety of organizations, including the Cornell Laboratory of Ornithology. The nonprofit Elderhostel organization offers excellent, reasonably priced, short courses for older adults. You might also want to take the famed home-study course in bird biology offered by the Cornell lab—details are at birds.cornell.edu/homestudy.

BANDING AND TAGGING

Bird-banding data are a crucial source of information about bird longevity, migration, and migration routes. Bands returned from such faraway places as France, Nigeria, and South Africa, for example, helped demonstrate the remarkable migration pattern of the Arctic Tern, proving that this bird makes an annual round-trip flight of 25,000 miles from its nesting grounds near the Arctic Circle to its wintering grounds in Antarctica.

Bird-banding operations in the United States and Canada are coordinated by the Bird Banding Laboratory of the U.S.

Fish and Wildlife Service; a special federal license and often state or provincial permits are needed to be an authorized bird bander. Volunteers are always welcome but are not allowed to handle the birds.

To band a bird, it must first be trapped, usually in a fine net called a "mist net." Each bird is carefully removed, identified, weighed, and examined for age, sex, and physical condition. A light aluminum band of the appropriate size is attached to the bird's leg, and the bird is released. Some 97 percent of all the birds banded are never found again, but the information provided by those that are recovered is invaluable. Very small birds are the least likely to be seen again, whereas up to 10 percent of banded game birds may be recovered.

If you find a dead banded bird (or if you find a band in a raptor pellet), remove it and straighten it out. To report the band, call (800) 327-BAND or go to reportband.gov.

If you find a band on a living bird, *do not* attempt to remove it—you might injure the bird. Carefully note the number on the band and release the bird, then report it as mentioned here.

In addition to banding birds on the leg, researchers sometimes tag or color-mark birds in other ways. You may see waterfowl or other large birds with conspicuous colored and numbered neck, wing, or leg bands. If you see a tagged bird, note the color and position of the tags, any visible numbers or letters and their position on the tags, and the general circumstances of the sighting. Report your findings to the U.S. Fish and Wildlife Service as mentioned earlier; also report your findings to the site office and local wildlife agencies. Tagging projects have a lot of possible sources; by reporting your sighting as widely as possible, you increase the odds that the individual bird or marking project can be identified.

Volunteering

Ornithology is one of the few sciences where the observations and assistance of amateurs are welcomed. Numerous bird studies, censuses, counts, and surveys are always being carried on throughout North America. The underfunded researchers in charge will often be glad to receive any help you can give. You don't have to know much about birds, but you do have to be enthusiastic, reliable, and willing to learn. Check with your local bird club, the biology departments of nearby colleges, local, state, and provincial wildlife agencies, and regional natural history organizations to find projects near you.

APPENDICES

APPENDIX A: AMERICAN BIRDING ASSOCIATION CODE OF BIRDING ETHICS

American Birding Association
Principles of Birding Ethics

Everyone who enjoys birds and birding must always respect wildlife, its environment, and the rights of others. In any conflict of interest between birds and birders, the welfare of the birds and their environment comes first.

Code of Birding Ethics

1. Promote the welfare of birds and their environment.

1 (a) Support the protection of important bird habitat.

1 (b) To avoid stressing birds or exposing them to danger, exercise restraint and caution during observation, photography, sound recording, or filming.

Limit the use of recordings and other methods of attracting birds, and never use such methods in heavily birded areas or for attracting any species that is Threatened, Endangered, or of Special Concern, or is rare in your local area.

Keep well back from nests and nesting colonies, roosts, display areas, and important feeding sites. In such sensitive areas, if there is a need for extended observation, photography, filming, or recording, try to use a blind or hide, and take advantage of natural cover.

Use artificial light sparingly for filming or photography, especially for close-ups.

1 (c) Before advertising the presence of a rare bird, evaluate the potential for disturbance to the bird, its surroundings, and other people in the area, and proceed only if access can be controlled, disturbance can be minimized, and permission has been obtained from private land-owners. The sites of rare nesting birds should be divulged only to the proper conservation authorities.

1 (d) Stay on roads, trails, and paths where they exist; otherwise keep habitat disturbance to a minimum.

2. Respect the law and the rights of others.

2 (a) Do not enter private property without the owner's explicit permission.

2 (b) Follow all laws, rules, and regulations governing use of roads and public areas, both at home and abroad.

2 (c) Practice common courtesy in contacts with other people. Your exemplary behavior will generate goodwill with birders and non-birders alike.

3. Ensure that feeders, nest structures, and other artificial bird environments are safe.

3 (a) Keep dispensers, water, and food clean and free of decay or disease. It is important to feed birds continually during harsh weather.

3 (b) Maintain and clean nest structures regularly.

3 (c) If you are attracting birds to an area, ensure the birds are not exposed to predation from cats and other domestic animals, or dangers posed by artificial hazards.

4. Group birding, whether organized or impromptu, requires special care.

Each individual in the group, in addition to the obligations spelled out in Items #1 and #2, has responsibilities as a Group Member.

4 (a) Respect the interests, rights, and skills of fellow birders, as well as those of people participating in other legitimate outdoor activities. Freely share your knowledge and experience, except where code 1(c) applies. Be especially helpful to beginning birders.

4 (b) If you witness unethical birding behavior, assess the situation and intervene if you think it prudent. When interceding, inform the person(s) of the inappropriate action and attempt, within reason, to have it stopped. If the behavior continues, document it and notify appropriate individuals or organizations.

Group Leader Responsibilities [amateur and professional trips and tours].

4 (c) Be an exemplary ethical role model for the group. Teach through word and example.

4 (d) Keep groups to a size that limits impact on the environ-ment and does not interfere with others using the same area.

4 (e) Ensure everyone in the group knows of and practices this code.

4 (f) Learn and inform the group of any special circumstances applicable to the areas being visited (eg, no tape recorders allowed).

4 (g) Acknowledge that professional tour companies bear a special responsibility to place the welfare of birds and the benefits of public knowledge ahead of the company's commercial interests. Ideally, leaders should keep track of tour sightings, document unusual occurrences, and submit records to appropriate organizations.

Please follow this code—distribute it and teach it to others.

Additional copies of the Code of Birding Ethics can be obtained from ABA. The ABA Code of Birding Ethics may be reprinted, reproduced, and distributed without restriction. Please acknowledge the role of ABA in developing and promoting this code.

American Birding

Appendix B: Birding Organizations

National Audubon Society
National Headquarters
225 Varick St., 7th floor
New York, NY 10014
(212) 979-3000
www.audubon.org

Public Policy Office
1150 Connecticut Ave., NW,
    suite 600
Washington, DC 20036
(202) 861-2242
www.audubon.org

National Science Office
545 Almshouse Rd.
Ivyland, PA 18974
(215) 355-9588
www.audubon.org

State offices and local chapters
of the National Audubon Society
are listed on the Web site at
audubon.org.

INDEPENDENT AUDUBON
SOCIETIES

Audubon Naturalist Society of the
    Central Atlantic States
Woodend Sanctuary
8940 Jones Mill Rd.
Chevy Chase, MD 20815
(301) 652-9188
www.audubonnaturalist.org

Connecticut Audubon Society
2325 Burr St.
Fairfield, CT 06924
(203) 259-6305
www.ctaudubon.org

Hawaii Audubon Society
850 Richards St., suite 505
Honolulu, HI 96813
(808) 528-1432
www.hawaiiaudubon.com

Illinois Audubon Society
2315 Clear Lake Ave.
Springfield, IL 62708
(217) 544-2473
www.illinoisaudubon.org

Indiana Audubon Society
Mary Gray Bird Sanctuary
3499 South Bird Sanctuary Rd.
Connersville, IN 47331
(765) 827-5109
www.indianaaudubon.org

Maine Audubon Society
20 Gilsland Farm Rd.
Falmouth, ME 04105
(207) 781-2330
www.maineaudubon.org

Massachusetts Audubon Society
208 South Great Rd.
Lincoln, MA 01773
(781) 259-9500
www.massaudubon.org

Michigan Audubon Society
6011 West St. Joseph, suite 403
Lansing, MI 48917
(517) 886-9144
www.michiganaudubon.org

Audubon Society of New
    Hampshire
84 Silk Farm Rd.
Concord, NH 03301
(603) 224-9909
www.newhampshireaudubon.org

New Jersey Audubon Society
9 Hardscrabble Rd.
Bernardsville, NY 07924
(908) 204-8998
www.njaudubon.org

Audubon Society of Rhode Island
12 Sanderson Rd.
Smithfield, RI 02917
(401) 949-5454
www.asri.org

OTHER ORGANIZATIONS

American Birding Association
4945 North 30th St., suite 200
Colorado Springs, CO 80919
(800) 850-2473
www.aba.org

Cornell Laboratory of Ornithology
159 Sapsucker Woods Rd.
Ithaca, NY 14850
(800) 843-2473
www.birds.cornell.edu

APPENDIX C: PERIODICALS FOR BIRDERS

The Auk
(505) 326-1579
www.aou.org

Birds & Blooms
5400 South 60th Street
Greendale, WI 53129
(800) 344-6913
www.birdsandblooms.com

Birder's World
Box 1612
Waukesha, WI 53187
(262) 796-8776
www.birdersworld.com

Birding
American Birding Association
4945 North 30th St., suite 200
Colorado Springs, CO 80919
(800) 850-2473
www.aba.org

BirdWatcher's Digest
Box 110
Marietta, OH 45750
(800) 879-2473
www.birdwatchersdigest.com

Living Bird
Cornell Laboratory of Ornithology
159 Sapsucker Woods Rd.
Ithaca, NY 14850
(800) 843-2473
www.birds.cornell.edu

North American Birds
American Birding Association
4945 North 30th St., suite 200
Colorado Springs, CO 80919
(800) 850-2473
www.aba.org

WildBird
Box 57900
Los Angeles, CA 90057
(213) 385-2222
www.wildbirdmagazine.com

The Wilson Journal of Ornithology
Wilson Ornithological Society
www.wilsonsociety.org

INDEX

ABOUT THE AUTHOR

Sheila Buff is a freelance writer specializing in both medicine and the outdoors. The author of *Insiders' Guide to the Hudson River Valley* and several books about birding, she lives in Milan in northern Dutchess County, New York.